MARGARET THATCHER

MARGARET THATCHER

Patricia Murray

W. H. Allen · London
A Howard & Wyndham Company
1980

Printed and bound in Great Britain
by W & J Mackay Limited, Chatham, Kent
for the publishers W. H. Allen & Co. Ltd.,
44 Hill Street, London W1X 8LB.

ISBN 0 491 02882 2

Contents

Illustrations

I would like to express my thanks to all the interviewees who have been very generous with their time and without whom the book would not have been possible. I would also like to thank Richard Ryder, and A. R. Mills for his editorial guidance.

P.M.

1

The Early Years

'But be not afraid of greatness;
Some men are born great;
Some achieve greatness,
And others have greatness thrust upon them.'
Twelfth Night, Act III, Scene IV Malvolio

On the morning of the 13th October 1925, Beatrice Ethel Roberts, nee Stevenson, gave birth to her second baby daughter. Margaret Hilda Roberts was born in the flat above their grocer's shop in North Parade, Grantham. Her mother originated from Lincolnshire but her father Alfred Roberts, hailed from Ringstead, Northamptonshire. His ancestry was Welsh on his father's side and Irish on his mother's. The potential Tory Prime Minister had none of the huntin', shootin', and fishin' ancestry which has dominated the Party for so many years. One grandfather was a shoemaker, the other a railway guard. Nor was there anything extravagant about the Roberts' household.

There was no garden, no bath or running hot water, and an outside toilet. Each bedroom had its own wash stand which consisted of a large jug and basin. The kitchen was very small and the furniture predominantly heavy Victorian.

Grantham itself is a typical small market town situated in the heart of the Lincolnshire countryside. Architecturally, it is dominated by the spire of St Wulframs, which is reputed to be one of the finest medieval churches in England. Historically, The Angel Hotel is said to be where Richard III signed the death warrant of the Duke of Buckingham in 1483. Charles Dickens praised the 18th century George Hotel when he described it in his book *Nicholas Nickelby* as one of the best inns in England. King's School was granted its name by Edward VI in 1553

9

and one of its most esteemed pupils was Sir Isaac Newton. The main industry is mechanical and agricultural engineering and Grantham being the nearest town to the RAF base at Cranwell, provides sanctuary and entertainment for the airmen who are stationed there.

It was in the atmosphere of this predominantly close community that the two girls were instilled with a strong feeling of duty and respect towards their parents, their elders, the church and their neighbours. The family unit was the focal point of their existence and as is the case with so many families, whatever difficulties befell one affected them all.

Margaret Thatcher has vivid recollections of her early childhood, perhaps more vivid than most. This may in part be explained by her parents' insistence on a very regulated pattern of behaviour and by their unwavering sense of duty towards the church and their neighbours. Mr and Mrs Roberts were described by the inhabitants of Grantham as people who were always true to their principles and beliefs. Margaret's father never tolerated the words, 'I can't' or 'it's too difficult', and although he set very high standards for one so young, his guidance was to prove invaluable for the years that lay ahead.

'We were a very close family and most of the things we did we tended to do together. My sister Muriel is four years older than I am so when you're very young that's quite a big gap and naturally our friends were very different ages, but even then we were close.

'Of course, if you have a grocer's shop, your father's work is very much a part of your life. We were a family grocer and in those days you used to go to people's doors, take down their orders and deliver the goods. My father went on the order round twice a week and sometimes I would go with him. In that era there was more to do in that type of shop than there is today in that you had to weigh up the butter from a large block, weigh out the sugar from huge sacks and weigh out the tea from tin canisters. All this had to be done on slack mornings and during the school holidays my sister and I used to spend many an hour helping our parents. We enjoyed this because there was always something to do and it made us feel rather grown up.

'My favourite time was undoubtedly the Christmas season when we put all the decorations up in the shop and I could hardly wait for all the crackers and Christmas cakes to arrive. It was a magical time and sometimes we used to spend the weekend packing up parcels for Rotary to send out to the old folk.

'Then I remember the great excitement when we bought the first delivery van. Cars weren't nearly so much a part of life as they are today and you had to work very hard to get them. It was quite an event when instead of having the goods delivered on a bicycle we actually had a van to go out with the orders.'

'What is your earliest recollection of serving in the shop?'

'I was about ten and I liked it because I met so many different kinds of people and came to know many of them very well. We used to stay open until seven o'clock on Fridays and eight o'clock on Saturdays. Thursday was our early closing day and my parents used to look forward to it all week. On Sunday mornings, my mother used to get up very early and do all the baking and by the time we all got downstairs at about eight, the first batch of cakes would already be out of the oven. She was a very, very capable woman. Before she was married, she had her own dress-making business. She never really had a moment to herself. She served in the shop, she did the housework, all the cooking, and washed and ironed all the sheets by hand. Nothing was ever sent to the laundry, everything was done at home – we had a big mangle and a dolly tub and my mother used to dolly things.

'My father did a tremendous amount of local council work. He was on the local council when I was about four so I can't remember a time when he wasn't. But it didn't stop there. Anything that required a voluntary helper he did. When we had National Savings, he assisted with that. He was an enthusiastic member of the Rotary Club, so we knew all about the work they did and he was on the Governing Body of both the girls' school and the boys' school. He was a voracious reader and from the age of about ten I used to go to the public library every Saturday morning to get out two books. He was on the libraries committee and naturally knew the librarian very well, so he would know exactly which two books to give me. There would probably be one on current affairs or a biography for my father and something of fiction for my mother.

'At the same time, I usually did the family shopping – obviously we didn't have to buy groceries but there were all sorts of things we needed from Woolworths and the ironmongers or the haberdashers. In those days there weren't as many multiples as there are now, the High Street was full of small shops which were all part of what was called The Chamber of Trade and all the shopkeepers knew each other very well. Accordingly there was never anything impersonal about going shopping, we asked after each other's families and the children all went to school together.'

Margaret's parents were both very religious and for years and years, they regularly attended the Finkin Street Methodist Church. Mr Roberts was a much sought after lay preacher and as well as all his other activities, he was a trustee of some ten other churches in Lincolnshire. That kind of religious dedication and awareness can have a considerable amount of influence on the whole family's daily life, so to what extent was Margaret affected by her parents' faith?

'Church work played quite a large part in our lives. I went to morning Sunday school at ten, then to the Church service at eleven, then to afternoon Sunday school at 2.30 where I was responsible for doing the musical accompaniment and generally to the evening service at six. Then there were a number of church activities during the week which we attended. My mother used to go to the sewing meeting on Wednesdays and there was the youth club on Fridays. I must say that belonging to a church as closely as we did meant that we had a tremendous number of personal friends. Every Sunday after the evening service, we would go back to supper with friends or they would come home to us. Having people from the church in to tea or supper was very much a part of our life.'

Mr and Mrs Roberts were described as caring parents who believed that their two daughters should follow a rigid code of conduct and Margaret has vivid memories of the form that discipline took.

'We had a very strict upbringing. We were never allowed to go to a cinema on a Sunday and we were forbidden to play any games such as snakes and ladders. Although there were playing cards in the house, we were certainly never permitted to use them on that day. Of course my grandmother lived with us until she died, when I was ten years old, and she was very, very Victorian and very, very strict. I think my parents probably insisted on some of these rules because they didn't want to offend her. My grandmother was forever telling us, "If a thing's worth doing it's worth doing well" – but you don't always take the advice,' she laughed. 'Another thing she always used to say, "Cleanliness is next to Godliness." Everything had to be clean and systematic. We were Methodists and Methodist means method. We were taught what was right and wrong in very considerable detail. There were certain things you just didn't do and that was that. Duty was very, very strongly engrained into us. Duties to the church, duties to your neighbour and conscientiousness were continually emphasised. My father constantly drummed into me, from a very early age, "You make up your own mind. You do not do something or want to do something because your friends are doing it. You never say well they're doing it, that's why I want to do it." '

'Was that a difficult practice to follow?'

'Yes, it's always difficult for children to be different from their friends or to do different things, to have different pocket money, or to do different things on a Sunday. However, it was very much the teaching my father followed throughout his own life. For example, a question which was raised at local council meetings for years was whether

13

or not the parks and the swimming pools and the tennis courts should be open to the public on Sundays. As an act of faith my father voted against it. In his view the Sabbath was not for playing games. But everything changed in war time, it had to and he couldn't have been more sensible about things. We had a lot of troops stationed around us as did everyone else and my father realised that it was very much better to have all the cinemas and games facilities open on Sunday so that the troops could relax and enjoy themselves as much as possible.'

'Most children love going out whether it be a visit to the fair or the local cinema. For some it's a fairly regular occurrence but for other's it's something of a rarity !'

'We didn't go out very much for pleasure. Of course in a shop a lot of the bookwork has to be done on a Sunday and church took up a great deal of our time, so when we did go out, it was on a Bank Holiday. But to go out somewhere, even to a cinema, was a tremendous treat and I used to look forward to it for days on end !

'Sometimes we went shopping in Nottingham, which was our largest local town, and I can remember one Bank Holiday going there to see a Ginger Rogers and Fred Astaire film. You see cinemas were so different in the thirties, they had large restaurants and some of them had brightly lit cinema organs which changed colours from blues to pinks to greens as the organ rose from the orchestra pit. The organist himself would generally be accepted as one of the personalities of the town in which he played and one of the most famous at that time was Sandy Macpherson who played the BBC theatre organ. Anyway, first of all we had tea, then we went into the cinema and listened to the organist and waited excitedly for the film to start. Afterwards, we went home by bus and I loved every minute of that day, which is probably why I can remember it so well. Nowadays of course you take these things for granted and they have lost a lot of their magic but to us going out was something which was viewed as a great treat in your life.'

Gillian Plumb who was at school with Margaret Roberts

described her as a rather serious girl. She attributed it both to her upbringing which was much more rigid than that of her friends and to the fact that her father placed a great deal of emphasis on academic pursuits.

'I *was* serious as a young girl. My father, as I have said, read a great deal. He had left school at thirteen, but he really had a first-class brain and was very, very talented. As a mother I know that you often want to give to your children the things you feel you yourself have lacked. My father lacked formal education and therefore he was most anxious that I should have every educational opportunity possible. Therefore anything that had an educational content was eminently desirable. That's why at the age of five, I was sent to take piano lessons, and I was always encouraged to do an enormous amount of reading. We used to have what were called university extension lectures, which involved visiting lecturers going to a school in the evening to give a talk on current affairs. I was taken along regularly every Thursday night to hear them speak. There was a music club about once a month where guest musicians played and we went to that. In fact we went to absolutely everything which was educational and cultural so naturally my friends would think I was serious.

'Talking of music, I shall never forget the first time we had a radio – it was a great occasion. I was about ten and went to a little primary school in Grantham – the Huntington Tower Road Elementary School. I can remember we had just over a mile to walk to school, a mile back to lunch, – there were no school lunches – then a mile back again in the afternoon and a mile back in the evening. One particular evening, when I knew we were going to have a radio – or what was called a wireless in those days – I was so excited that I ran practically the whole way home. It opened up a whole new world for me. I always listened to *Monday Night at Seven*, to Arthur Askey and Richard Murdoch in *Band Wagon*, and to *Saturday Night Music Hall* which presented all the star names of the day. Then there was a programme called *ITMA* and one of my favourite characters was Mrs Mop the char lady, played

15

by Dorothy Summers, whose catch phrase was, "Can I do yer now sir?"

'One of the later characters and I believe one of the few surviving members of *ITMA* is Derek Guyler and it was the first time I really became aware of that Liverpudlian accent in his portrayal of Frisby Dyke. Another favourite was Jack Train as the alcoholic Colonel Chinstrap, whose tag line was, "I don't mind if I do sir." There really was an enormous number of variety shows in those days and we knew them all. During the war years there was always a postscript after the nine o'clock news – sometimes Winston gave it and on other occasions it would be given by J. B. Priestley, A. P. Herbert or Quentin Reynolds who was a famous American journalist. Then there was a marvellous programme called *In Town Tonight*. The whole family used to listen to that on Saturday and I don't think there's ever been a better programme of its type.

'The radio formed a very large part of our lives. We all loved big band music. There was Ambrose, Roy Fox, Harry Roy, Lew Stone and Jack Payne. Henry Hall, whose signature tune was 'Here's to the Next Time', was the best-known orchestra of those times. He was heard more than the others because he was the director of the BBC Dance Orchestra and I particularly liked his *Saturday Night Guest Night*. During the war years Geraldo came to the fore and when I was in my early teens I listened to Mantovani. I always listened to Victor Sylvester because he taught dancing – "slow, slow, quick quick slow" – and I loved the romantic melodies and superb lyrics of Jerome Kern, Cole Porter, Irving Berlin, Richard Rogers and Lorenz Hart.'

At the age of eleven, Margaret won a scholarship to the Kesteven and Grantham Girls School. Her sister Muriel was already a pupil there but Margaret's scholarship didn't cover the full fees. However, her parents were more than willing to make any sacrifices that were necessary for their daughter's education and through various economies they found the extra money. Margaret did very well at school and according to her mistresses and school-

16

friends not only did she excel academically but she had a real sense of fun and possessed a natural ability for sport. Her schoolfriend Gillian commented, 'In spite of her many talents she didn't evoke any feelings of resentment among the other girls, because she wasn't an exhibitionist, nor was she the bossy type. In fact she was a rather quiet unassuming girl who was generally well liked. We were in the same hockey team together, the first eleven, and we never lost a match.'

From all accounts Margaret had a very full life at school and despite her friends' comments and the fact that she was the youngest girl ever to be selected for the hockey team, she still insisted that Muriel was much more sports inclined.

'We were both taught to swim at the age of about three and I enjoyed all the team games such as hockey and net-ball but unfortunately I was never very much good at tennis. I've always regretted that because you only need two players, so you can make arrangements at the last minute and it's a marvellous game to play with family and friends.'

'What particular subject interested you at school?'

'I was interested in all the various subjects but we were very lucky because we had good teachers and I think that liking a subject so often depends on how interesting a teacher makes it. I found art difficult, my interest in that has come later in life, and I wish that we'd placed more emphasis on learning languages. Naturally we learnt French, but it was only when I wanted to go to university that I had to be taught Latin. Latin wasn't taught in our school which was a pity because it really is a marvellous basis for other languages. We had a very good history teacher but the subject was taught as a series of events and I think that if you have been in Parliament and have tried to take a small part in making contemporary history then you start to look at the decisions your forebears have made in a slightly different and a much more sympathetic light.

'Of course the rise of Hitler came in the thirties and my sister and I used to hear our parents discussing it. We all had pen friends at school, my sister had one in Austria and I had one in France. My sister's penfriend was actually German and I vividly recall the day we received a letter from her parents asking whether we would have Edith to stay with us if they managed to get her out of Vienna. This was after Hitler went into Austria – Edith was a Jewess. Thank God we managed to get her over and she came to live with us. She would talk to us for hours about all the things that were happening so we learned from her about the dreadful things that were going on there.

'Then when I was thirteen, my sister left home to go and take a course in physiotherapy and naturally I missed her a great deal.

'As I grew older, I had difficulty in choosing whether to go on the science side or the arts side and in those days you had to decide at about fifteen, soon after you had done your matriculation. You either took all science subjects or all arts subjects. I think I know what decided me and I'm sure it's been the same with a lot of young people. We had a marvellous chemistry teacher, a wonderful teacher and a wonderful person and I'm sure that that decided me to take chemistry which I did. Also science was the coming subject and it was expected that there would be a lot of opportunities in research. By the time I had reached the sixth form, I was of course already doing science and my father had become mayor. He was sitting on the bench as a JP and whenever I was free during the school holidays I went along to the court with him. One day my father took me to have lunch with the Recorder (a Recorder is a lawyer and presides over the court) and I had a long talk to him. Having listened to all the various cases in court, I realised that I was really becoming fascinated with law and wished in a way that I could have done law, but I couldn't because I already had my university entrance for chemistry. However, he told me not to worry, apparently he had taken a physics degree, so he advised me to take my chemistry degree and then to do law in my spare time – there's a large area of the law where both qualifications are necessary, namely the patent bar.'

Margaret's schoolfriends described her as an exceptionally good debater and one suggested that she may have known even as a child that her ultimate destiny lay in politics. But what were her ambitions as a schoolgirl – were politics involved?

'No. Politics as such weren't involved in any way at all in those days but I certainly enjoyed debating and belonged to the debating club at school – but politics, no. I can, however, remember my first experience of politics which was in the 1935 election. I was only ten but I remember it very vividly. The whole family used to go to the committee room and help and the only way in which I could help was to run like mad between the committee room and the polling station to get the lists of the numbers of people who had voted and then check them off. It seems so strange to me now, but it was quite a thrill for those of us who worked in the committee room when the candidate Victor Warrender came round to talk to us and of course it never occurred to me that one day I would be in the same position. But as far as actually going into politics was concerned – no! There was absolutely no question of it because I couldn't possibly have afforded it! In those days, people weren't paid very much for being in politics. I think they were paid about £400 a year with no secretarial help, so it could just not have been contemplated ever! It was beyond my vision because I always had to think in terms of a career in which I could keep myself.

'I did do quite a lot of amateur acting at school which I enjoyed and at one stage I really would have liked to have been an actress but don't forget to me it represented a sort of glamorous life which was almost unknown. There was a contact, however, because among our customers were some people called Campbell – Mr and Mrs Campbell, who were very well known locally. They owned the picture house in the high street and they had a theatre which put on repertory plays and pantomimes. Their daughter Judy Campbell went on to the stage and made her name in a show called *New Faces* where she sang *A Nightingale Sang in Berkeley Square*.

'I had wanted from a very early age to go to university but looking back on it all I think I was probably pointed in that direction. The opportunity to go to university was to us a chance almost undreamed of. My father had never done it, but it was assumed that I would try to get in somewhere and the subject was clearly marked out for me. Oxford and Cambridge were then just worlds that I'd heard of.'

According to Margaret's headmistress Miss Gillies, she had very determined views for a young girl. As an example of that determination, she crammed a five-year course of Latin which she needed for her university entrance into a year and incredibly when she took the exam, came out top. She then sat for a scholarship at Somerville College, Oxford but despite all her efforts and hard work, she suffered a real setback. In her particular group, there was only one award available and although she was equal first on all the papers, the other girl had waited a year to sit for the scholarship and it represented her last chance. In the circumstances the authorities awarded her the scholarship and gave Margaret Roberts a bursary. Unfortunately this didn't cover all her fees and residential expenses but once again her parents rose to the occasion and somehow managed to scrape the money together.

'My parents always made sacrifices for my education – always. There was never a great deal of money at home and we always had to be very careful, that's the only way I can put it.'

'Some people in Grantham who knew your father very well felt that he tried to realise his ambitions in you. Is this a view which you share?'

'Yes, I think he did try to realise his ambitions in me. He hadn't had an education and therefore he was absolutely delighted that I was able to go to university. You see when I brought up my children, I tried to give them more things that were enjoyment and entertainment. When I was a child we didn't often go out to have fun together, but I suppose my parents just didn't have very much spare time

– they believed that it was wrong to spend very much on personal pleasure.'

'Later, as a teenager, did you have the opportunity of doing more fun things, such as dancing, or was the accent still on purely cultural pursuits?'

'I don't think I ever went to a dance until I went to university. Dancing was frowned upon by my parents – dancing was forbidden. I was allowed to learn ballet and eurhythmics because that was cultural, but everything always had to have some cultural content. In those days, our pleasure was really confined to church socials – but don't forget a tremendous social life does revolve around the church. There are supper evenings, singing evenings, spelling bees and that's what our social life really consisted of. We used to go to tea with the minister's wife, which was fine, and I suppose it was only just at the back of my mind that my life revolved completely around the church whereas others had different fun. But don't think it was dull, it wasn't. However, not many of my schoolfriends did those things so in a way I was cut off from them.

'I can't really remember going out a lot for fun. As I've said, it was rare even to go to the cinema. But on one occasion, I really was given a fantastic opportunity. I was sent to London to stay with some friends of ours who lived in Parliament Hill Fields. I stayed for a whole week and was given a life of enjoyment and entertainment that I had never seen!'

Margaret Thatcher's face lit up as she remembered that magical week.

'I was taken all over London to see the various sights like the Changing of the Guard, the Tower of London, the zoo and I can well remember that we were actually taken to the theatre – to a musical called *The Desert Song*. We saw the crowds and the bright lights and I was so excited and thrilled by it that I've never forgotten that week. Otherwise we went to functions of the town which were very pleasant and functions of the church. But I suppose again in those years, we were being shown in the odd film a life which doesn't really exist for anyone. No one I know

21

of has a glamorous life – I don't think it exists.'

'Looking back over those years, do you feel that perhaps there was something missing in your youth in that you didn't have as much fun, or the same kind of fun as your other friends?'

'I think most of them went out for pleasure more than we did.'

'Did that concern you?'

'Well, I think you only mind if your friends have it and you don't and it makes you different from them. I was different in those days, I was more serious. When I went to stay with my great friend Jean Farmer, they all went to tennis together. They all went to dances together. They would all do far more of those things – out with other people where there was laughter and fun!'

'Would you have enjoyed that side of life?'

'Yes I would. We always went to serious things, or our laughter and fun was at the church social. It wasn't at the village hall where everybody had a dance.'

'When did you first become interested in those all important teenage pursuits such as clothes and make-up?'

'Having an elder sister meant that I was introduced to everything before she was. Muriel went to Birmingham for five years to study physiotherapy and she learned and told me about a life that I had never known. Although she only received a very minimal pay, she soon discovered how to make the most of it and where to find the best buys in clothes. You see we had always had things made at home and for us it was an unbelievable luxury to go out and buy something off the peg. As I've said my mother was a very good dressmaker but my sister and I often felt that our things were different from others. Actually our things were really very pretty and beautifully made. Muriel soon found her way around the big city shops and my knowledge of make-up really began when she started to give me the odd glamorous thing for Christmas such as a powder compact. It all stemmed from there.'

Margaret Roberts spent a great deal of time with her father and several people commented that she may have been closer to him than she was to her mother.

'I think I probably was closer to my father but my mother was a good woman who was always intensely practical and I learned a lot of practical stuff from her. She taught me how to cook and bake bread, how to make my own clothes and how to decorate. We always used to decorate our own home because we could never afford to have decorators in and I've always liked doing things with my hands.

'She was very proud of her home and everything in it was as shiny as a new pin. It was always important for my parents to buy good things, therefore we would go to sale-rooms and buy good mahogany furniture. It seems incredible to think about it now but in those days you could pick things up so cheaply. For instance I remember on one occasion that we decided against buying some mahogany chairs for the dining room because they went for the outrageous sum of £1 each. Everything we bought was always second-hand because my parents didn't think that modern furniture was very well made so they went for the craft things. When we bought a second-hand settee and chairs, my mother, in spite of all her other chores, covered them. When I think back on it all, it really was astonishing how hard she worked and it's sad to think that she rarely ever had time to sit down. You know children don't really appreciate how hard their mums work until they get older and some of them become mums themselves. She was a particularly generous lady too. When she had done all the baking, she would always send off cakes or whatever we happened to have to anyone who was either ill or who wasn't very well off. Some of our friends were unemployed and what we had we shared with them.'

Mr and Mrs Roberts based their lives on hard work, self-reliance, honesty and a deep-rooted concern for their fellow human beings. These were their guiding principles which they instilled into their two daughters. But there was another principle that Mr Roberts considered to be of the utmost importance.

'The toughest thing of my childhood was that my father

taught me very firmly indeed, "You do not follow the crowd because you're afraid of being different – you decide what to do yourself and if necessary you lead the crowd, but you never just follow." Oh that was very hard indeed but my goodness it has stood me in good stead.'

'Would you describe your childhood as a happy one?'

'Yes I would . . . I would.'

2
The Old Girls' Reunion

I am not the first person to write a book on Margaret Thatcher, but at least I have the rare distinction of being the first biographer to go to the Old Girls' Annual Dinner of the now famous Kesteven and Grantham Girls school. It was held at the The King's Head Hotel and judging by the turn-out was a very popular event on the Grantham calendar.

The evening began with drinks at the bar and a chance to renew old friendships and catch up on all the local gossip – a commodity which judging from the buzzing conversation, was in plentiful supply. The tones were all so well modulated – not a trace of a Grantham or Lincolnshire dialect dropped from the lips of any of the old girls. Their speech was positively Thatcheresque. I was greeted by the present headmistress Miss Pannell who hospitably offered me a drink. I offered to return the compliment and on being refused produced a packet of cigarettes. 'Do you smoke?' I asked. 'Oh no!' replied Miss Pannell. 'Do you mind if I do?' I mumbled tentatively. 'No, but I'll have to move away from you,' came the brisk reply.

The gathering found its way into the starkly lit dining room where three long tables were bedecked in pure white linen tablecloths. We had a choice of starters, melon cocktail or fish cocktail followed by a chicken casserole with peas, carrots and potatoes. To the consternation of the ladies sitting next to me I declined the vegetables and the cry went up – 'What no peas!' – 'No carrots!' – 'No potatoes!' – 'All very good for a growing girl my dear!' The meal was eventually rounded off by large portions of meringue gâteau and generous cups of milky coffee, all very nicely served by smiling waitresses. Throughout the course of the evening, I grew increasingly aware that I was the object of some suspicion and perhaps a little curiosity. I tried to answer each momentary look with a smile – sometimes the smile was returned but on other occasions it was met with a blank uncompromising stare. I do not suffer from a persecution complex and their uneasiness and reticence was certainly understandable. After all, it was an intrusion on their privacy and it was very good of the school to allow me to be there.

Towards the end of the evening, there was something of a disturbance when it was suddenly discovered that the glasses had been inadvertently removed before the Loyal toast. Jugs of water and fresh glasses quickly appeared and Miss Pannell rose to propose the Queen's health. She subsequently made a speech welcoming the girls of yester-year and then paused for a moment to glance in my direction. 'Mrs Tricia Murray is here with us tonight and she is married to a *disc* jockey – I suppose some of you here will have heard of him. Apparently she is going to write a book on Margaret Thatcher.' She paused again and I was immediately aware of another sideways glance. She con-tinued, 'I do hope though that she will forgive me when I say that it seems to me that everything both fact and fiction has already been written.' I managed a smile and tried to look composed by nonchalantly sipping a glass of vintage water. I had just emptied the contents of the glass when she went on, 'However, there may be someone here who was at school with Margaret and who could perhaps talk to Mrs Murray afterwards, though as we are already running very late, I expect that most of you will want to dash off home.' The speech ended with a resumé of school news and then Miss Gillies, who was headmistress in Margaret Thatcher's time, rose to bring the gathering up to date on her past years' activities. Miss Gillies, who was born in Perth, is un-doubtedly a very witty and amusing speaker. She delighted her audience with tales from Scotland and I gratefully joined in the laughter. As they say in the best detective stories, the heat was off. Two other speakers followed, gave news of absent friends, talked of Christmas cards received and the evening drew to a close. I was suddenly overcome by a feeling of panic; there wasn't a moment to lose. I hurriedly went to retrieve my note pad and looked hopefully around the room for someone who looked as if she might have been at school with Margaret Roberts. Thankfully, I was approached by Hazel Burton who had been in the same class as her from the age of eleven to sixteen. Hazel, a very friendly animated lady, was in the midst of recounting some of their past exploits together when several other ladies appeared on the scene. 'Don't you say that, don't write that down, cross that out – we've been misquoted before you know, they echoed as one. But Hazel whose enthusiasm was understandably dampened, ploughed on gamely and continued with her early reminiscences.

'Margaret always looked immaculate at school. Her mother who was a poppet and very shy took a great deal of pride in making sure that the two children were well turned out. It's quite untrue to say that Margaret has put on airs and graces since she left Grantham – she was always well groomed. She was top of the class and I was generally near the bottom but we were great friends and used to share a garden plot together. We had what was fun in those days and I can remember as if it were yesterday how she used to walk back to school after she had been home for lunch clutching a small bar of chocolate. Every day without fail she would share out that chocolate right to the last little piece. She was very generous and shared whatever she had with anyone who happened to be around, even though she had very little herself. Perhaps it seems a silly little story to remember but in those days we didn't get much money from our parents to buy sweets and it was something of a treat to have chocolate.

'Margaret always did everything very well and apart from the academic side, she was good at sport and singing and other school activities. This may have led to a feeling of resentment among some of the other girls who were a bit envious of her many talents but Margaret was just genuinely enthusiastic about whatever she did and never displayed that irritating characteristic of showing off. She was very close to her father and whilst he was essentially

27

a gentle man, he appeared to be very strict with his two daughters and he influenced and encouraged Margaret a great deal. In the light of everything that has happened, it's interesting to recall that she was a very good speaker even as a little girl – an attribute which is unusual in one so young. She was always very sincere, meant exactly what she said and was never afraid to ask the question "why?".' Hazel had only been speaking for a couple of minutes when I became acutely aware of an all pervading silence in the dining room. I looked up just in time to see the furtive figure of Miss Gillies disappearing through the door. Making my apologies to Hazel, I rushed out to see if I could find her but it was too late. I returned somewhat crestfallen and one of the remaining gathering remarked – 'I don't think Miss Gillies wanted to speak to you' – she went on to explain why. Apparently several people in Grantham felt that they had been badly misquoted in the past and that several of the things that they had said had been taken out of context. They were so upset by past experiences that they were automatically suspicious of any new inquisitor.

The ladies' room which as any self-respecting female knows can be the centre of local gossip, was my last hope. There one or two of the late-leavers who had lived in Grantham all their lives talked readily and enthusiastically about the corner grocer shop run by Mr and Mrs Roberts. It was a shop that could be relied upon for its good quality food, its immaculate condition and its courteous service. But it was more than that for it appears to have been something of a local meeting place and very much a part of the community. The Roberts were described as gentle, friendly people, who had a kind word for everyone. Mr Roberts who was a Methodist lay preacher took a very active part in local life and was undoubtedly a very popular and well respected figure. He was described as tall and distinguished with iron-grey hair and the bluest of blue eyes. He obviously made such an indelible impression among the inhabitants that they found it difficult to realise that he was no longer with them. The lights in the cloakroom dimmed

and the last of the ladies scurried out. The Old Girls'
Dinner was over for another year and so it seemed were
my chances of talking to anyone else who had shared those
bygone years with Margaret. But as Mr Micawber used to
say, 'Something will always turn up,' and it did in the
shape of a lovely grey-haired lady who put her head warily
round the cloakroom door and whispered, 'Miss Gillies is
staying in Grantham overnight. Perhaps you could pluck
up the courage to track her down in the morning. Do you
think you dare?' she asked tentatively. 'Yes,' I murmured.
My mind was made up. A good night's sleep and I would
be on the trail again tomorrow.

The day began with a long talk to Margaret Goodrich
(now Margaret Wickstead) who has known her namesake
from the age of about fourteen right up until the present
day. Margaret Wickstead who appears to be very down
to earth with an essentially warm outgoing personality
talked quite uninhibitedly about her life-long friend who
incidentally is two years her junior.

'I was first aware of her when I was in the fifth form.
She was in a class below but she caught my attention then
because she was a very clever little girl who was quite
unafraid unlike the vast majority of girls to ask questions
at the end of a public lecture. She used to stand up and put
her question in a very parliamentary fashion starting with,
"Does the speaker think this or that?" She could use words
correctly at a far earlier age than most of her schoolfriends
and she seemed to know more about the world at large
and what she wanted to do than most of her contemporaries.

Time passed and it wasn't until sixth form days
that their paths really crossed. 'We were then both part
of a very good hockey team and Margaret, who was an
extremely good player, played regularly at centre-half.
Those were memorable days in school and everybody in
the team were great friends and had a lot of fun together.
During this period, we both attended biology classes and
dissected many a dog fish together in the lab. I always
had the impression that Margaret was interested in

politics and in retrospect its interesting to contemplate that she may have felt even then that she was ultimately destined to go into Parliament. Her father whom she absolutely adored probably inspired this particular interest because he was an active town councillor and later an alderman. He was a very able man who had left school at the age of thirteen but he would undoubtedly have had a university degree given the present day educational opportunities. He had a great deal of influence on her life and perhaps tried to fulfil his ambitions in her. I remember Margaret telling me on one occasion that her father would never tolerate expressions such as: "I can't," or "I don't think I can manage it," or "It's too difficult." Everything was a challenge and she just had to cope with it. If it was difficult, then there was all the more reason for doing it. However, Margaret was always prepared to work extremely hard. Hard work is her God and she can work all the hours that he gives.'

But schooldays were beginning to draw to an end and whilst Margaret Goodrich was about to go up to Oxford, Margaret Roberts was working hard to get into university. She too badly wanted to go to Oxford but even more importantly she wanted to go to university *somewhere*. Margaret Goodrich recalled how her father helped Margaret to get a place at Nottingham but then out of the blue Somerville, whose waiting list she had been on for some time, sent a telegram saying that there was after all a place for her at Oxford.

'When Margaret arrived at Oxford, I had already been there for about two years and she was just like any other shy girl from a town like Grantham. I can remember visiting her with my father in Somerville and there she was sitting, toasting crumpets and feeling very homesick just like any other fresher away from home for the first time in her life. Although in later months she was to become well known in the Conservative Club, she certainly went through a patch of feeling strange and lonely among her unfamiliar surroundings. During those years, she frequently visited us at Corbey Glen and she would always

30

arrive with a bag of groceries for my mother. She never came empty-handed.'

As she was reading chemistry, Margaret Roberts didn't have nearly as much free time as some of the other students.

'But whatever free time she had, she certainly made the most of. University life opened up a whole new world of opportunities for both of us. She enjoyed sport, sang with The Oxford Bach Choir and in her third year became Chairman of the Conservative Association which involved entertaining Cabinet Ministers on Friday nights, hearing them speak at the Union and generally looking after them.'

'But what about those all important female pursuits such as boyfriends, clothes and make-up?'

'I didn't really know much about Margaret's boyfriends at Oxford because we were in different colleges but I vividly recall a funny little incident which occurred on my 21st birthday. Margaret arrived at my party carefully nursing a carnation which she had been given by her current boyfriend. She was absolutely determined to keep that carnation alive and frantically searched among my books to see if she could discover any chemical which would preserve it. But the search proved to be fruitless and in the end the carnation had to settle for a glass of water and an aspirin. I think the carnation survived but I'm not too sure about the boyfriend. As far as clothes and make-up were concerned, she couldn't buy anything at all when she was at Oxford because she didn't have any money. Of course it was war time and there was very little in the shops to choose from.'

Although the two Margarets went their separate ways after leaving Oxford, they remained in close contact with each other and Margaret Goodrich remembered the period when she was teaching in Hertfordshire and spent most of her free time in London. 'Margaret would never let me spend any money on food and lodging and always insisted that I should use her flat whenever I was in town. She has always been very hospitable and thoroughly enjoys doing her own cooking. I think she probably missed not being able to take many of her own friends home when she was young. Her parents were always so busy in the shop and I remember that I only went to tea with her once to the many times she came to us. Ever since she became a young woman, she has more than redressed the balance.'

Over a span of some forty years, Margaret Wickstead has come to know her illustrious friend intimately and she described her most predominant characteristics in this way, 'I have never met anyone with Margaret's infinite capacity to work. She has always been and still is, incredibly well organised. I don't think she could survive if she wasn't. She has always been capable of running a house, bringing up a family and doing a job of work and has done all three things extremely efficiently. The pressures of being a housewife and mother can't be measured in the way that hours of work at an office can and she knows exactly what it's like to be a wife and mother and what it really means to have to do the shopping, cook all the meals, look after the children and run the house. I can remember calling on her just before they moved to their present house in Chelsea and there she was going round with a whole pack of stick-on labels so that there wasn't a single packing case left without a label on it. Suddenly she decided that we ought to have some coffee and as we sat there drinking coffee and guzzling chocolate biscuits, she looked up and said – "Hasn't God been good to us – aren't we lucky not to have suffered with any of those illnesses which afflict so many people as the years go by."

'As well as being highly organised, Margaret is very practical. If a curtain fell off a hook, she wouldn't wait for somebody else to put it up, she would do it herself and when it comes to decorating, she knows exactly how to plaster a ceiling or paper a wall. She's so full of energy and gives the impression that she is enjoying whatever she happens to be doing at that particular moment. She has never in her life had time to sit around and moan and wish that she was doing something else. She is a very courageous

32

With the twins, Carol and Mark; a treasured picture from the family album

A wedding-day photograph: Margaret Roberts, soon to be Mrs Thatcher, with her father

Above: Carol and Mark aged six; *below:* with the twins in 1958

person who is quite prepared to have a go at anything. It would be impossible to talk about Margaret without mentioning her generosity which is an integral part of her nature. She has always been very, very generous. If she had things that you hadn't, she would be the first either to give them or to lend them. She is sympathetic and possesses that rare ability of being able to feel with the people that she is with and of understanding their problems.'

'Success has an uncanny habit of changing people for the worse. Faced with the unprecedented achievement of becoming the first female leader of a main political party, in Great Britain, has Margaret Thatcher succumbed to success and allowed it to go to her head?'

'No, quite the reverse. So far she has matured and improved and is a more likeable person to the general public. To me she's much the same as she ever was for even though she has travelled a long way from her Grantham days, she and Denis are always most anxious to hear all the local gossip whenever I see them. It's invariably the first topic of conversation. No I don't think that in any way success has gone to her head. She is a nicer, warmer person and only time will tell whether she will prove to be the exception to the normal rule.'

Having conducted an intensive search, Miss Gillies's whereabouts were eventually located. She was staying with a friend and although she appeared to be very reticent to talk to me, she finally agreed to the interview provided I promised to make it brief.

Miss Gillies, who is in her seventies, is a strikingly robust character who takes a lively and somewhat amused interest in today's rapidly changing world. She welcomed me with a broad smile and whilst we sat munching toast and drinking tea she talked about the schoolgirl who had become a household name. 'She was undoubtedly one of our outstanding pupils and came top in her class in every year except one. She was always ambitious and very eager to learn and her father encouraged her in everything she did. He was chairman of the school governors and as headmistress I worked closely with him. He was an energetic, industrious man who made a considerable contribution to the community life of Grantham. He was well known among most of the inhabitants and figured prominently in the local gatherings. His wife was a much quieter person who I think preferred to stay at home but she was very kind and considerate and a source of great strength to her husband. Mr Roberts doted on Margaret and he used to spend many an hour with her talking about politics. She was perhaps closer to him than she was to her mother but they were a very united family.

'However, it would be wrong to assume that Margaret was preoccupied solely with academic pursuits and serious discussions to the exclusion of everything else. She was a good all-rounder and very keen on sport. I seem to remember that she became the youngest ever captain of the girls' hockey team and enjoyed playing anything from netball to tennis.

'Of course society has changed significantly since the last war but in Margaret's schooldays it was still very much a man's world. But far from being deterred by the possible pitfalls which may or may not be encountered on entering a male domain Margaret's reaction was to comment, "Don't you think it makes it all the more of a challenge Miss Gillies?"

'When the time came for her to go to Oxford, I was asked to give her a reference. On looking through her school reports, I was fascinated to see the phrases: "she is a very logical thinker", "she has a very clear mind" repeated time and time again. I believe that logic and clarity of mind are two of her great qualities today. Such attributes are unusual in a schoolgirl but I believe that she was sowing the seeds of her ultimate destiny even then. I am not at all surprised that she has got to the top but as a former headmistress of a different generation, I'm sure you will understand when I say that it's rather like being in the middle of a scene from *Alice in Wonderland*.'

At this juncture, in strode Miss Pannell who seemed somewhat surprised to see me. 'So you're still here in Grantham,' she observed disapprovingly. 'Of course as I told you last night, I didn't know little Margaret Roberts, that was all before my time. However, she did visit the school in the Spring of last year and I must say the girls were all very excited about it. It was quite extraordinary you know, they even stopped whilst in full flight on the netball court to wave to her. Quite frankly though, she did respond extremely well to the girls and seemed genuinely delighted to be back at school again. When she eventually left it caused quite a commotion, I can tell you. All the girls in the various classrooms actually stood up and charged to the windows to wave their goodbyes.' It was now the turn of Miss Pannell to come to a halt whilst in full flight. She stared at me suspiciously and a look of impending gloom flashed across her face. She made a supreme effort to conceal her misgivings, managed a faint smile and said, 'I do hope you're not going to come up to the school and start taking pictures with all your long-haired friends from the BBC. We've had all this before you know. Last time there were cameras and reporters everywhere. I've never seen anything quite like it. It totally disrupted the school curriculum for the whole day.'

'Didn't the girls enjoy it?' I asked meekly.

'Oh yes, they were virtually falling over the banisters trying to get into the photographs.'

I did my best to assure her that I would not be invading the school with or without my long-haired friends and decided that the time had come for my departure. After all the mistresses had been very hospitable and I had intruded on their privacy for the second day in succession.

'Well, I don't think there's any more we can tell you,' they said pointedly. '*You are going back to London to-night, aren't you?*'

I detected a high note of optimism. 'Yes,' I replied, 'thank you for your time.'

'Drive carefully my dear, it's a long way for a youngster to drive on her own . . .'

35

3
Oxford

Margaret Thatcher once said, 'Oxford and Cambridge were just worlds that I'd heard of,' but in 1943 she too was to become part of that world. The principal of the college for part of her time there was Dame Janet Vaughan who is renowned for her work on bone structure and her research into blood diseases. An exceptionally distinguished member of Somerville College was Margaret Roberts's chemistry teacher, Dorothy Hodgkin, who subsequently won the Nobel prize for chemistry in 1964 and is the first woman since Florence Nightingale to have received the Order of Merit.

'I went to university when I was seventeen, it was war time and we were all urged to complete our courses in technical subjects because the country needed people who were qualified technically. If I had waited until I was eighteen I would have to have taken the shortened degree because women were called up at twenty.'

Most of the students were older than Margaret Roberts, some by several years, because many had served in the war prior to going to Oxford. There were very few girls in those days studying chemistry but it wasn't a conscious desire to go into a man's world which prompted her to enter that field, it was simply that her talents pointed her in that direction. Scientists had a much more arduous timetable than Arts students. Every morning and most afternoons were spent buried in the laboratories and when they finally emerged, it was to attend early evening lectures.

Although she started her working day at about 6.30 in the morning, she wasn't able to join in the fund of university life until the evening. But whilst she earned a reputation for being an extremely hard worker, she didn't confine herself to purely academic pursuits. According to her friends, she had a real capacity for enjoying herself, took an

36

enthusiastic part in college activities and was able to enjoy a life which was quite different to anything she had experienced at home. For the first time in her youth, she was able to go to dances.

Despite a very full life at Somerville, all was not immediately at its best in those first few months.

'I was always rather homesick. When you've been at home, you have never known what it's like to be lonely, it's quite an experience the first time you come across it and it takes a while to make new friends. Yes I was homesick. I think there would be something very wrong with your homelife if you weren't just a little...'

'What particular aspect of university life held a special fascination? Was it the political clubs?'

'I joined the Conservative club right from the beginning simply because I was interested but it was really no more than that. Whatever club you joined, there was an eventful life revolving round it and most of the students joined one or more of the associations. But what particularly interested me was the opportunity of meeting an enormous amount of people from vastly different backgrounds.'

Although Miss Roberts's time was predominantly devoted to her scientific studies, her father's unwavering dedication to voluntary service had left an indelible impression on her mind and she regularly worked twice a week in the Oxford forces canteen, making sandwiches and washing up. During the vacation, she invariably returned home to Grantham and in 1944, she took a part-time teaching job at The Grantham Central School for Boys. As money was in very short supply, it provided the ideal opportunity to supplement her funds and feeling somewhat affluent, she treated herself to a bicycle.

When war ended in 1945, an election was called and the University Conservative Association took a very active part in the Oxford campaign which was between Quintin Hogg and Frank Packenham. It was quite a long campaign which was held partly during term time and partly during the vacation and Margaret Roberts took a fairly vigorous part. 'I remember canvassing some of the streets

37

in Oxford, some of them have gone now, some of the worst housing areas have thankfully disappeared. I also attended various meetings and the first real election meeting I ever went to was in the town hall where Quintin was speaking. Then when term ended, I went home and took part in the Grantham campaign. By that time I was nineteen and I used to go round the town doing quite a lot of speaking which I must say I enjoyed.' The results of the election were announced and the Conservatives were shattered by their overwhelming defeat : Labour had a majority of one hundred and forty-six in the House of Commons. 'We were all absolutely shaken by the outcome of the 1945 election. To me it seemed utterly unbelievable that the nation could have rejected Winston after everything he had done . . . fantastic . . . unbelievable . . . However, the Labour Party *were* in Government and for the first time members of Parliament were paid a living wage. Their pay was increased immediately to £1000 a year and from that moment on it became possible to think in terms of a political career.'

'Was it at that precise moment that the thought of a parliamentary career first crystallised in your mind?'

'Actually, I can tell you exactly when the thought first crossed my mind. Several of us went to a birthday party given by one of Margaret Wickstead's friends in Corbey. At the end of the evening, we all finished up in the kitchen and somebody who happened to be talking to me said, "I feel that what you would really like to do is to be a member of Parliament," and that was the very first time that it had occurred to me that perhaps one day I could, if the chance ever came. However, I was still at university and knew that my first priority when I came down was to earn my own living and get established.'

Margaret Roberts graduated with a second class honours degree in chemistry and many years later, in 1970, the college bestowed on her the highest honour they had to give, an honorary fellowship of Somerville.

Her first job on leaving Oxford was in the development section of a plastics factory in Manningtree, Essex. Stanley

38

Booth, who was in charge of research projects at B X Plastics, commented : 'We were never a chauvinistic firm. We employed quite a number of women even in those far off days. They were there on merit. Margaret, the scientist with a second, was very thorough and whilst she wasn't the most imaginative chemist, she ran rings round most of the men. But even in those days, her eyes were set on a distant political horizon. It didn't surprise me at all when she won the leadership of the Party, she's head and shoulders above the lot of them in the House. Let's face it, how many politicians can you name who could hold down a place in industry as she did ?'

Although Margaret Roberts was interested in her job and liked the people she worked with, those around her were well aware that her interest in politics hadn't waned. She took digs in nearby Colchester and immediately joined the local Conservative Association. Two years later she took the opportunity of going to the Party Conference and that's where her long uphill struggle on the road to Number 10 really all began . . .

4

Always Dartford

Life is full of unpredictables. A casual conversation or a chance meeting can lay the foundation for one's future. Such a meeting took place in 1948 and eventually resulted in Margaret Roberts being adopted as the Conservative candidate for Dartford.

'I usually went to Conservative Party conferences either representing the Oxford Conservative Association or later the Oxford Graduates Association. One day I travelled from Colchester to the conference at Llandudno and a great friend of mine, John Grant, happened to be sitting next to John Miller, the Chairman of the Dartford constituency. John Miller remarked that they were looking for a candidate to which my friend quickly retorted, "Would you consider a woman?" "Oh no," came the immediate answer, "Not a woman! Dartford is an industrial seat." "Don't turn it down out-of-hand," replied John, "At least meet her first. She's only young, twenty-three and for a difficult seat like Dartford, a woman might just be the right thing." '

In those days, it was much more difficult for a woman to get into politics than it was for a man and the situation today is certainly not one which could be described as offering equal opportunities. Margaret Roberts was the only female candidate on the list but once the committee had seen her, there was never any doubt and they whole heartedly adopted her — she was the youngest woman candidate in the country.

But Dartford had another very special association for Miss Roberts which stretched far beyond the realms of politics, for it was there she met the man who she was ultimately destined to share the rest of her life with. One of her supporters was a Major Denis Thatcher who was the managing director of a family paint firm in Erith. He had served in the war in France, Sicily and Italy and was awarded the MBE and mentioned in dispatches. She vividly recalls their first encounter. 'I first met Denis on the night I was adopted as candidate. You're chosen by a Selection Committee, then you have to be presented to the whole association to be adopted and Denis was very friendly with some of the people who were active in the association. There was a meeting at eight o'clock and then I had to give a speech and answer questions. Afterwards, I naturally wanted to meet and talk with as many people as I could but there was one problem. How in the world was I going to get back to Colchester from Dartford so that I could be back in time for work the next morning? Luckily Denis came to my rescue and drove me to Liverpool Street where I caught the very late night train to Colchester.'

Having been selected, Margaret Roberts agreed to live in the constituency. She had to give up her job in Manningtree and find something in the London area. She worked then in the laboratories of J. Lyons & Co. at Cadby Hall in Hammersmith doing research into food and food technology. She took digs in Dartford with Mr and Mrs Woollcott and was lucky to find such a kind and considerate couple. She lived with them for almost two years and Mrs Woollcott clearly remembers her stay there. 'Margaret used to get up shortly before 6 a.m. and left the house regularly at 6.35. She used her bedroom as a study and fought both elections from our house. She often worked in her room late at night and seldom turned the light off before 2 o'clock in the morning. She had a fantastic amount of energy, I won't say that I've never seen anyone like it but she certainly takes some beating. She had a very hectic time in Dartford because the constituency covered a wide area and she had her fair share of traumas. The village hall was the scene of one of her first political speeches and she had scarcely uttered a word when the electricity failed and the room was thrown into total darkness. But far from being ruffled or bad tempered, she just laughed and chatted away whilst candles were lit. She was always a chatterbox. When you have somebody living with you seven days a week, you see them in their true colours, and however tired she was, things never seemed to get her down. She was always cheerful and I can honestly say I never heard her grumble even though there was very little time for fun in her life. She had very simple tastes and for want of a better expression, there was never any side to her. She didn't have many clothes in those days but she always took great care of them. I remember she had one special black velvet dress which she always wore when she went out in the evening, and I can see her now standing over the ironing board in the kitchen desperately trying to steam out all the seat marks. Despite her elevated position, she has never changed towards us and we always knew that if we needed her help she wouldn't hesitate to give it. A few years ago, we had a difficult legal problem. We went to two lawyers but they were unable to resolve it, so we decided to telephone Margaret. She told us not to worry and within days she had sorted out all the issues. Apparently the other side just caved in.'

Lord Pannell who at that time was Chairman of the Dartford Labour Association commented that when Margaret came home after a long day's work, she would start another full day's work in the constituency.

'I used to catch the 7.10 to Charing Cross and the 6.08 back, then I would get a bus home, have a quick meal and go out either for an evening's canvassing or to an evening meeting. I would normally return home about 11 p.m.'

'Was it ever too much?'

'Yes sometimes perhaps it was, but the great secret of life is really turning 90 per cent of it into habit. In that way you can keep it turning over – after all you don't think about cleaning your teeth, it's a habit.'

Lord Pannell's view is that it was usually the practice of the Tory Party to send new candidates into Labour strongholds to win their spurs and demonstrate their stamina and ability. He felt that, despite almost impossible odds (Labour had a majority of 20,000 in 1945), Margaret worked the constituency with all the drive, determination and enthusiasm of a potential winner.

'But why devote so much time and energy to an almost insurmountable goal?'

'We were still rather shocked by the 1945 result and felt that it should never have happened and it was our bounden duty to swing it back in 1950. The recent by-election results had been very good (majorities of 19,000 had tumbled to about 6) and we really thought that we might conceivably do it. We didn't of course, it came down to about 12,000 but there's nothing like being an optimist when you're young. If you're not an optimist when you're young then you'll never be one!'

'And now?'

'Yes I'm still an optimist but I'm a much more measured one now. You must be an optimist to carry on, to have a certain approach to life but as you get older you become a more measured one. You have a better assessment of what is possible and what is probable and you acquire more stamina as you get older, you learn to take your disappointments much better. Naturally there are times when you get depressed but tomorrow is always another day and I'm always hopeful!'

Although Labour easily held on to the seat in 1950, their majority had been reduced by a third and the Conservative vote had increased by 50 per cent. From all accounts Margaret Roberts had deservedly earned the reputation of being an indefatigable worker. She went out canvassing relentlessly, whether the venue was the factory gate, the workers' canteen or the local butcher's shop. She never turned down an invitation to speak provided she was able to get there on time after a day's work in London. Perhaps not surprisingly, the Dartford Association had no hesitation in re-adopting her as their candidate and as a token of their appreciation for all her efforts they presented her with a marcasite brooch. 'I really wanted to stay in Dartford for another election and it was obvious that there was going to be one before long. By that time I knew so many people and had so many friends and we all worked together. In tough seats, and I'm sure both political parties find this, you get the most marvellous band of helpers and a tremendous bond of friendship develops which stays with you all your life. I wanted to stay because of the people. You know you really do stay in a place longer because of the people – you really do ! In fact it's a danger with many of our young candidates now that they will stay on fighting very difficult seats which some of them haven't a hope of winning – they stay there because they don't like to let the people down. Sometimes you have to say to the committees, "If you find a really good candidate sticking to a very difficult seat, you'll eventually have to pull him out and say we need you in Parliament." There are three or four now who would be superb here but you don't like just to move them – you can't – but sooner or later they will have to change their allegiance.'

Although the election was keenly contested by both parties in 1950 and 1951, Margaret Roberts remained on very good terms with the sitting MP Norman Dodds and the campaigns were fought in a very congenial atmosphere. Neither party indulged in any personally malicious remarks and people on both sides have alleged that the young Tory candidate never brought personalities into politics, a principle which from all accounts, she has strongly adhered to throughout her political life. After the 1950 result, Norman Dodds took her to lunch at the House of Commons and on another occasion, they were both guests at a civic ball at Crayford Town Hall, where according to the *Evening News*, 'They were to be found gliding across the dance floor in perfect harmony.'

'I remember that evening very well. Norman was there as the MP and I was there as the Conservative candidate. He asked me to dance and just as we stepped on to the floor it so happened that the band started to play a tango called "Jealousy" ! Norman was always very kind and courteous to me. We had great debates together but we always had a great respect for one another. There was never any nastiness at all – never.'

As anticipated, the election took place in October 1951

44

and Miss Roberts's birthday happened to fall during the campaign. Much to her surprise and great delight, the party workers celebrated the day by sending her bouquets of flowers and the women of the division presented her with a hatbox and weekend case. As one such lady commented, 'They say women don't like other women, but I don't think that's basically true; she was very popular with women.'

Labour, as expected, held on to the Dartford seat, but Margaret Roberts had a different kind of triumph, she had won the heart and respect of all those who had worked with her. She had served her apprenticeship in a tough seat but her direct involvement in politics was to lay in abeyance for another seven years for on the eve of polling day, much to everyone's surprise, Denis Thatcher announced their engagement.

5

At Home

On 13th December 1951, Margaret Roberts married Denis Thatcher at Wesleys Chapel, a Methodist church in the City of London. It was a bitterly cold foggy day and the bride wore a long sapphire blue velvet dress with a matching hat trimmed with a grey osterich feather. 'I was determined to be warm and I wore it as a dinner dress for a long time afterwards. I've still got it somewhere but it's all scuffled up.' The couple spent their honeymoon in Lisbon and Madeira and returned to live in Chelsea, only just across the road from where they are living now.

It's difficult if not impossible to arrive at a true impression of a person's private life unless you see them in their home surroundings. The House of Commons scarcely lends itself to an informal chat about family life. The home environment isn't exactly in evidence amidst the corridors of power. The inner confines of the House itself were described by Woodrow Wyatt, in the *Sunday Mirror,* as a cross between the London Palladium and an all-in wrestling tournament.

It was with this in mind that I went to see Margaret Thatcher on a sunny June evening, her first free or relatively free evening in six weeks. Their home is a modest detached house just off the Kings Road and the door was opened by a smiling Denis Thatcher. There is nothing sombre or heavy about the Thatcher home, quite the reverse. Walking into the hall was rather like walking into the sunshine, for it's decorated in a rich glowing coral colour. The dining room, study and kitchen are situated on the ground floor and the sitting room and bedrooms are upstairs. Mrs Thatcher, who was waiting at the top of the staircase to greet me, showed me into the lounge. The immediate impact was one of warmth and cosiness. Although the house is situated in the heart of London it takes on the aspect of a country home. The sitting room is small with magnolia walls, a central fireplace, green carpet, and chintzy country style furniture. There are no paintings or portraits simply a photograph of Carol Thatcher taken by her mother when they were in China. It's a real home in every sense of the meaning. Perhaps, surprisingly, there are no traces of Westminster in view except for one solitary picture which hangs in the dining room depicting the legendary characters of the day such as Gaitskell, Wilson, Atlee, Churchill, Macmillan and, sitting right at the back, a smiling Mrs Thatcher. There are no real signs of the hustings of Parliament here. Despite the obvious pressures of public life the Thatchers have managed to maintain a family identity.

Denis Thatcher offered me a drink, and Mrs Thatcher settled back into a chair, kicked off her shoes and talked about those early years as a wife and mother. I asked her what particular aspect of her new role as a housewife had she particularly enjoyed?

'I had always loved cooking, and being at home gave me the opportunity to experiment with new recipes. Of course it's very hard work being a housewife, apart from all the daily chores, there's the laundry, the shopping, the break-fast to get, the midday meal, tea and supper. However, in a way you have more of your life under your own control – all right you've got to get meals ready at certain times but you can decide what you're going to do next, what you're going to have to eat, how you arrange your room and who you're going to invite home. One of the things I enjoyed most of all was having the opportunity of entertaining, of having people in for supper.'

'Do you still find time to do the cooking?'

'I always cook breakfast and get the meals ready when-ever I'm home. Otherwise I prepare something so that the family can help themselves. None of us lead very regular lives – we eat at odd times. I never quite know who is going to be in for lunch and who is going to be in for supper but there's always something that we can all cut at in the fridge.'

47

Prior to getting married Margaret Thatcher had enrolled as a student at Lincoln's Inn. She had always wanted to take up law and she continued her studies whilst she was at home. Two years after her marriage, in August 1953, she gave birth to twins, a boy named Mark and a girl named Carol.

'I had the children the day we won the Ashes – *do* I remember. It was a Saturday and we couldn't find my husband anywhere. The twins took rather a long time to arrive and *he* had mooched off somewhere.' Incredibly, only four months later, she took her bar finals and qualified as a barrister. 'I thought that if I didn't do something quite definite then there was a real possibility that I'd never return to work again, so I entered my name for the bar finals. That was really an effort of will because I felt that unless I made it, I would just tend to give it all up and therefore it was almost a challenge to really get stuck into it. When the children are very tiny, it's very exacting because they need a lot of feeding and there's a lot of washing but I was lucky because I had help.

'The interesting thing to me having had twins is that they are born with different personalities – they just are. Their personalities were obvious almost from the first day they were born and they were very, very different. Twins are either quite unalike or very similar and if they're not identical, and a boy and a girl can't be, then they tend to be very different, as Mark and Carol were. Although I started practising at the bar when they were a year old, I was never far away – my chambers were only about twenty minutes from home, so I knew I could be back very quickly if I were needed.'

'Were you able to spend much time playing with them when they were young?'

'Oh yes, I played with them a lot. I just wouldn't have missed it, and that's why I would think it impossible for a mother with young children to be an MP if she lives way out of London. She wouldn't see them for two or three days and she'd feel that she was missing so much. When children are small, you have to handle them regularly because they recognise the *way* you handle them. I remember on one occasion going away for a fortnight and leaving the twins with my mother. When we came home, it took them about a day to get used to my handling again – it was quite astonishing.'

'Most mothers are perpetual worriers but some adopt a more *laissez-faire* attitude towards their children.'

'I worried all the time and of course ninety per cent of the time you worry about things that don't happen – but you still worry! You bring them up carefully and then they catch everything – they just do. Actually it's better that they do catch these complaints when they're young because they get it over with, but you don't think so at the time when you're all packed up to go away on holiday and one of them gets chicken pox and you have to cancel it. Both of mine had mumps at the same time and as I'd never had it as a child I naturally caught it. You just have to go through this stage – you just do. There are times when you think you are never going to get any real sleep again. Mine being twins, they wanted feeding regularly. You go through a period when they want a late night feed, then they're up early in the morning. Of course young children are always up early and if you've been up late at night, you begin to wonder whether you are ever going to get a decent night's sleep again. But suddenly you're through it all and then it's very difficult to get them up at all.'

'Did you stay up at night when they were ill?'

'Oh yes, and you become a very light sleeper – the first cry and you are awake and in their room in a flash. I think children are afraid of the dark and for a very long time, I would always leave a light on in the hall landing with the door open, or I would make sure there was a small night light of some kind. There's no point in trying to make them get used to the dark, most children are afraid of the dark and it's much easier for them to have a very dim light so that they can just wake up and see that everything is all right.'

'How much of a disciplinarian was Margaret Thatcher?'

49

'I wasn't very strict – medium so really. You have to tell your children what's right and wrong and you must obviously have some rules but you don't want rules for the sake of rules and you must explain them. They ask endless questions and you need endless patience but you have got to explain, you've got to try and give them answers. One of the great problems today is that some parents don't talk to their young children enough. Now I was lucky, I had someone in to help with the twins and I was told how important it was to talk to them. When you pick them up and bath them, there should be a continuous round of chatting. Of course mothers are always busy and there are a lot of pressures but you have to try and find time to explain things. Every day from tea time to bath time was spent with the children. However, not every mum can do that by any means. It's not so much the actual time you're with them but how much attention you devote to them during that time.'

Although Margaret Thatcher had a strict religious upbringing, certainly by today's standards, her children weren't brought up in the same religious environment.

'When we lived in a village, we used to go to a children's service in the village church. At a later stage when they both went to boarding school, they attended Chapel on Sundays. Whenever parents were allowed to visit Denis and I used to go up to their school and go to the service with them, but after that I did not insist that they went to church. I think that was probably because I'd had so much insistence myself.'

Her own parents had placed a great deal of emphasis on cultural and educational pursuits, did she introduce her children to a broader spectrum of entertainment?

'It was mixed really. As I've said, when I was a child we seldom went out to have fun together and you tend to try to give your children things you hadn't had and we took them out very much more. But I did encourage them to go to most things. After all, we lived in London and it seemed an awful pity not to take advantage of every opportunity. However, I did know that if I were to say to them, "Now,

50

on Sunday afternoon we're going to an art gallery," instead of being pleasurable, it becomes educational. But I think they've got to know where to go so that in due course, if they want to, they can go themselves. And Carol is certainly very keen on visiting art galleries. We took them to the theatre to see different types of plays and we introduced them to the opera. We really tried to introduce them to everything so that they could then choose for themselves what they wanted to do.'

'A lifelong friend has commented that you didn't have parties as a child. Did that apply to Mark and Carol?'

'No, we gave a fair amount of parties for them at home and then they would go to those given by their school-friends.'

'Did the twins suffer when they were young as a result of your career?'

'No I don't think so. I became a Member of Parliament when they were about six and it just became a part of their life. But I was lucky because I had a London constituency, a London home and I was working in London but it's a rare combination. I think when they're older they tend to suffer more because they are much more in the public eye and that's very tough on them, very tough! I think the greatest difference between now and my younger day was that auntie or mum often lived in the house or just next door or around the corner and therefore if mother was out at work, there was always some other member of a different generation of the family to be there when the children came home. Formerly, two or three generations of the same family used to live in the same house or the same town or village. Fortunately quite a number of people still do because that gives an area its stability. But I do believe that someone should always be there when the children are due to come home. However I appreciate how difficult that may be for some people.'

'What is the key to combining a successful career with a happy family life?'

'The key is linked with the personalities themselves. You can't do it unless you all fit in together. It has to be organ-

51

ised and everybody has to agree that you do it. You can't lay down any hard and fast rules. You've got to build the rules around the personalities.'

How important is the family to Margaret Thatcher?

'Vital – absolutely vital! A happy family life makes the world of difference to a person and blood is thicker than water. It's a two way business. You are always there for them whatever happens to them and they're there for you whatever sort of day you've had. You can accept criticism from your family which may sometimes be difficult to accept from others. Home is a place you go to and from which you go out. When you have your own children, it's the first time in your life that you really live for someone else in a way you never have before. What happens to them matters far more than what happens to you and it's a totally different depth of experience!'

6
Life At The Bar

Margaret Thatcher started life at the Bar as a pupil in common law chambers at King's Bench Walk which had a large criminal law practice. Later, she was to go into tax chambers and Peter Rowland takes up the story.

Peter Rowland is a tax specialist and international lawyer. He first met Margaret Thatcher in 1955 when the then head of chambers, introduced her into the set at King's Bench Walk and suggested that Rowland should be her pupil master. (Pupillage is a type of apprenticeship which every newly qualified barrister serves.) Apparently Margaret Thatcher had met the head in 1954 and he had promised to sketch out her career at the bar. He had advised her to do three different sets of pupillage in various chambers. The idea was to give her all round experience so that when she came to the tax bar, 'she would have a better background than virtually anybody else there' (apart of course from a technical background). He had asked her to do her final pupillage in his chambers and then to stay on as a tenant. Naturally she was delighted with the idea.

'Margaret was my first pupil and she was the only woman in chambers. The revenue bar is a specialised field whose particular function is to advise tax payers. There are only about forty practising members of the genuine revenue bar and women usually decide to go into divorce and criminal chambers. So far as I am aware, even to this day, there are only two female practising members of the Tax bar.

'Margaret was my pupil for six months, she was serious, hard working, eager to learn and not to teach her masters. She was a good scholar and never closed her mind to other people's views – far from it. She was keenly interested to find out what other people thought. If she didn't agree with them, she kept her own counsel. I don't know whether she disagreed with some of the things I said but if she did, she put it in a most tactful way so that I wouldn't realise I was being put right. She's quite a diplomat. Margaret didn't mix very much with other members of chambers after hours, she didn't go to the pub for a drink, because she was anxious to go home and be with the twins. But she was always easy to get on with.'

Those were happy days for Margaret Thatcher, but just when her future looked assured her hopes and expectations were shattered.

'After she had been my pupil for six months, the head who was a very difficult man in many ways and became more difficult at this stage, changed his mind about her altogether and she simply was not offered a seat in chambers which she had been promised. Consequently, Margaret had no alternative but to go, which was very unfair in my opinion and very much against the wishes of other members of chambers. I don't think his decision had anything to do with her as an individual. He was a very strange man and for reasons which I can't explain he just decided that he would contract the chambers and that's all there was to it. (It's impossible to practise at the bar unless you're a member of chambers.) He was very much in control as many but not all heads of chambers are. He and the senior clerk decided in a rather peremptory fashion that they would limit the number of members and would not find a place for her. He could perfectly well have done so and everyone thought she had been very shabbily treated but no one could do anything about it. She was very worthwhile keeping on because she was bright, keen to contribute and given the experience her opinion would have been highly valued. As a person, she was liked and respected and we all wanted her to stay on.'

We all have to face and learn to live with whatever setbacks life unfolds, there isn't really much alternative. But how did Margaret Thatcher react to what must have been a bitter disappointment?

'Very well outwardly. Goodness knows what she thought but there were no scenes or tantrums, or anything like that. She never made it a public issue. She didn't ask me if I could do anything for her because she realised she just had to accept it. She knew that with the head of chambers and senior clerk united on a course of action, there was nothing that could be done. But I knew from the occasional look which appeared on her face in unguarded moments that she was extremely disappointed.'

'Were there any harsh words levelled at the head?'

'No, she was very generous to him. I think if I'd been her, I would have been inclined to call him a few things. After all he made a promise, then broke his word for reasons that were wrapped up in his personality. But I don't remember her issuing any criticism against him which was greatly to her credit. In retrospect, it may well be that the senior clerk had some anti-female feelings. He was a clerk of the old school and I don't think he felt that a woman would really make a success in tax chambers. Indeed, it is difficult to do so, it's essentially a male domain. The sort of cases that revenue lawyers usually deal with are important cases which have already been considered for a period of anything from six months to three years by a substantial firm of accountants and/or solicitors. The clerk would probably have asked himself, if a person had had all this advice and then came to counsel as an ultimate arbiter, would he have sufficient confidence in a woman. Whereas a person will go to a woman on a complicated issue involving divorce or crime, when it comes to looking at accounts a lot of people don't have that confidence in a female lawyer. It's totally irrational but unfortunately it's true even today.'

'Was Margaret Thatcher aware that she was entering a male preserve?'

'Yes, she knew that she would encounter a certain amount of prejudice but she felt it was a challenge and it may well be that that is what attracted her.'

A lot of water has passed under the bridge since those far off days of 1965 and Peter Rowland has kept in touch with his one time pupil ever since. But how much has success changed her?

'From what I've seen and know of her, far from everything going to her head, I think it's had exactly the opposite effect. I don't think success has spoilt her at all. I think she's become more human rather than less. She was a little reserved at one time but she's more outgoing now. She's always been very natural and the fact that she's become a very successful MP hasn't made her the least bit pompous, which is very unusual.'

'What particular facets of her nature have enabled Margaret Thatcher to be one step away from the summit?'

'Very hard work, intelligence, diligence and a pleasant personality. She's not abrasive in the sense of being mean-minded or difficult. She doesn't make unkind or malicious remarks about people so I doubt whether she has made many enemies apart of course from political ones or those who are jealous of her success. Although from what I've heard in the House of Commons, she gives as good as she gets in debates, I am sure she would never mount a kind of smear campaign which other politicians are quite capable of doing – it's just not in her nature . . .'

Having left King's Bench Walk Margaret Thatcher joined a set of tax and chancery chambers at 5 New Square, Lincolns Inn. But whilst she enjoyed her practice at the bar, her sights were set on Westminster.

In 1955, she tried unsuccessfully to be adopted as the candidate for Orpington and later she applied for nomination at Beckenham but once again she ran second. She was naturally disappointed, but she always had to try for seats near home because she was adamant that she would never leave her children overnight.

But in 1958, her luck changed and she was adopted as the candidate for Finchley, having been selected from two hundred applicants. Finally, when she was elected, she gave up her practice at the bar. 'You can do two jobs in life but you can't do three. You can run a home and be a Member of Parliament but if you try to do all three, you will end up by doing none of them well.'

In 1959 Margaret Thatcher entered Parliament, but not even in her wildest dreams, or most ambitious moments, could she have foreseen the developments in her political career and the future that lay ahead.

7

My Mother

Twenty-five year old Mark Thatcher, a chartered account-
ant by profession, is the son of the most famous female
commoner in Britain. He has a ready smile and appears
to be relaxed, indeed even untouched by the drama that
goes on around him. But is he? What are the pressures of
family life now?

'They're just to maintain as well ordered a family life as
possible – to go about my business in a perfectly normal
way but above all not to put any unnecessary pressure on
mum; not to bother her with little things like, "the laundry
hasn't come back this week." To make her life so easy that
the family life just happens; to always be there when you're
wanted and not to be around when you're not. It's very
hard to analyse the pressures on all the family because
there are different pressures on different members. I know
what the pressures are on me and try to support mum as
much as possible.'

'Does she still see herself as a housewife?'

'She's never stopped being a housewife. If I have friends
in for lunch, she insists on preparing it. Not just two
courses, but the whole bit. She really enjoys it. She always
wants to do these motherly things whenever she can.
She's fantastic.'

'How much opportunity is there to discuss family problems. Do you and Carol go to her with your worries?'

'She's always there whenever we need her which is the
most important thing. She loves family life. I feel she probably regrets that we haven't been able to have as tight a
family life as others. I too regret that we haven't always
been able to discuss family matters but on the other hand
that's one of the disadvantages to set against the many
advantages. We all tend to be quite independent. We make
our own decisions, particularly Carol. She's a free and

easy girl and tends to keep out of the limelight. It all really stemmed from the time she was at university. During that period, mum was Secretary of State for Education and Carol had rather a rough time. She was at a very impressionable age and I think it hit her hard. She was a bit overpowered by it all. She wants to establish her own identity and it's something you have to work at, but you get there eventually. I think she's frustrated at being labelled as Mrs Thatcher's daughter as opposed to Carol Thatcher. But whatever she does, as long as she's happy, we as a family will always help her and she's very happy now working as a journalist in Australia. Prior to that, she followed mum into law and qualified as a solicitor. Carol loves travelling and she's been all over Europe, all over North America, to Japan, Hong Kong and to China with mum. She's happier being more independent, and that's fine.'

'Despite all the outside pressures, are you basically a close-knit family?'

'Oh yes, yes. As soon as something goes wrong, we all close ranks immediately. In times of crisis we are all there for each other. We are a very close family in our own way.'

'To what extent if any was your childhood affected by your mother's career?'

'It didn't really affect my life at all when she became an MP in 1959 because prior to that she had gone out to work every day. The fact that she changed from law to politics didn't make any difference. In fact I very well remember the day she was elected walking into the garage and seeing the car covered in blue ribbon and confetti. I couldn't quite work it out because the car had never looked like that before but even though I was only six, I can remember thinking, "she's really going places".'

'When did you become aware of the enormity of your mother's position?'

'It was in 1970 when she got a place in the Cabinet. It really started to effect me then. I was beginning to grow up and understand what it was all about.'

Margaret Thatcher had a particularly strict upbringing. Did this influence the way in which she raised her own children?

'No, we weren't brought up very strictly. It was a sort of back scratching operation. If I did the things she expected of me as far as work was concerned and behaved in a reasonably civilised fashion, it was fairly easy going. If I misbehaved or did something idiotic, then it was trouble just as it would be with any mum.'

Mark Thatcher's mother knows what it's like to live with criticism. Politicians are constantly under attack. They accept it with varying degrees of sensitivity as part of the job. But what about the family and in particular the son, how susceptible is he?

'I tend to look at who is making the criticism before I assess it. After a year, you soon find out who's for and who's against – those who are against just keep on sniping. But it's all part and parcel of the job and I've learnt to develop a thick skin on that subject – you have to. I get more upset when she gets upset – we all do. If it's grossly unjustified and it really goes to the bone as far as she is concerned then I get unhappy because I don't like seeing her unhappy.

'There are several types of criticism. There's genuine political criticism from politicians, there's journalistic criticism which is their job and you accept it. Then there's criticism from people who know nothing about politics though they think they do and that's just sour grapes. Then there's a fourth category which is genuine criticism from those who know and understand and want to help. One to three just bounces off, category four, you've got to listen.'

How sensitive is your mother to these shafts?'

'She used to get hurt easily. That milk episode shook her. She almost went the colour of shamrock. She was quite young as far as Cabinet ministers go and it gave her a bad name in the public eye for a good year, quite wrongly in my view. I think she did the right thing because it gave her the opportunity to reallocate the twenty-two million pounds to other educational programmes.'

Stamina is an essential prerequisite of any politician. But according to people from both sides of the House, Margaret Thatcher's powers of endurance are legendary.

'She's got a constitution like an elephant! She works phenomenal hours. She's the lady who never sleeps. When the heat is really on, she gets about four hours. Normally if she goes to bed at 2, she'll be up between 7 and 7.30 to get the breakfast. That's the family's regular daily meeting – it's not exactly sparkling at that hour in the morning but we all find out each other's plans for the day.

'There are lookers and doers and she's the original doer. If the furniture has to be changed round, she doesn't wait for anyone to move it, she gets on with it herself and when it comes to decorating, don't even talk about it. She hasn't got time now, but in the past, she would come home and say, "I don't like the colour of this room," and she'd just do it – wallpaper the lot. At our last house, she wallpapered three or four rooms – half the joint. If she puts her mind to anything, however difficult it is, she'll do it. Whether it takes, ten hours, ten weeks, ten months, or ten years, she'll do it. She won't stop till she's finished.'

Has this built-in determination applied throughout her political life? Has it been one of the main factors in enabling her to stay the course?

'Oh yes. Her determination is quite extraordinary. She carries this determination to everything she does. She believes very strongly that we can get out of this mess and I think she also believes that if the country is going to be a better place to live in, it will get there a lot faster with her at the helm. That's not a boastful summation in any way. She passionately believes in what she's doing. She has to because it's a very hard course – it's a way of life. She's lucky she enjoys doing her job. The fact that it's a job is secondary, she'd do it for nothing. The trouble with being the Leader of the Opposition is that you're always thinking negatively, you're always knocking things down. You're not creating, which in itself is slightly soul destroying, but you work for the day when hopefully you're on the other side of the fence.'

61

How often does the temper get frayed? How low is her boiling point?

'I can see when the ends are getting frayed and you know you've got to back off for a bit, it's just like lighting a blue touch paper. Like most people, when she's very tired, small things irritate her. The degree of anger or irritation is related entirely to how hard she's working or what pressures she's under, which is natural. But whenever she loses her temper, she gets over it very quickly.'

When his mother wants to get away from politics, what does she turn to? How does she relax? What makes her laugh?

'She really has very little time for leisure these days but she thoroughly enjoys watching the two Ronnies – they always make her laugh. We went to see them at the Palladium only recently. They have a degree of subtlety to their humour. There are many others she likes too, such as Morecambe and Wise, and Eric Sykes to mention but a few. Mum laughs a lot at home. She enjoys light entertainment. She has a broad taste in music but unfortunately she doesn't get enough time for it. She likes taking exercise and on a sunny summer's afternoon, she enjoys walking for half an hour, just looking at everything and taking it all in, but the opportunities are very few and far between and as she never has the same free hour the same week, she can't make any arrangements to play sport. She likes reading, is interested in political biographies and collects porcelain. She's a woman of very simple tastes and very simple values but she has good taste.'

Does the family have many evenings out together?

'I can count on one hand the number of times the whole family has been out for a meal together in the last four years. I love to sit down and have a quiet family dinner but we can only have that at home now. On summer evenings, we often used to wander down the King's Road (Chelsea) looking in all the shops to see what clothes were kicking around. Not any more. If we do that now, we have to have an army of detectives going with us. Those things have all gone. Basically, under it all, we're just a normal family.

We have normal values and we like doing the things which everybody else does. However, there are so many ordinary things we are no longer in a position to enjoy so much – but there we are – '

Having a mother as party leader obviously puts the spotlight on the whole family. How does Mark Thatcher react to the situation?

'When she was elected, it was a source of very great pride to me – God I can't tell you how proud I was. The press however had found a new toy for a couple of months and I soon learnt that I had to be very careful. One evening I went to a restaurant with some friends and took along a girl who I'd known for some time. Afterwards, we went on somewhere else for a coffee and I picked up the first editions of the newspapers. Wham! I was horror struck, there on the front page was a large picture of myself and this girl walking into the restaurant. Of course, she did her nut and I can't blame her. I'm so careful now, I'm practically a teetotaller. If I got done for speeding the press would have a field day.'

'Have your friends changed towards you?'

'Some think I've changed and have moved away from me a bit. Well I suppose I have changed in a way but only to accommodate the family environment. If mum's got an evening off, I try to be in. Some people think that just because I'm Mrs Thatcher's son, it's plain sailing, but it isn't because at the end of the day I've got to earn my own living like everyone else and have my own life. Broadly speaking though, my close friends tend to be the ones I had before it all started. They understand.'

Who does he take after?

'I'm more like my mother in many ways but I'm very close to dad as well. Dad has a rough time because of the demands on my mother. He's a very strong personality. He was very successful in his own sphere. Now he has to sit back and play second division. That's naturally very hard for a very proud man and takes an awful lot of doing. But he's totally 100 per cent for mum. He does and would do anything he could to help her. Carol tends to keep out

63

of it as much as possible and I just slide along in the middle but we're all utterly loyal.'

How does it really feel to be the boss's son?

'I lie in bed thinking about it. I can't believe my mother is who she is. For the first six or seven months after it happened, I used to think, "What makes me so special to be the son of the leader of the Opposition. I've done nothing to deserve it, nothing at all." I realised that suddenly I was in a different league where I was expected to behave in a certain way otherwise I'd get crucified by the world outside. So I try and fulfil other people's expectations of me.'

And if she became Prime Minister?

'Naturally we will have to forgo more family life and be given more responsibilities but even so I will happily pay the price. I will be filled with enormous pride and enormous humility!'

And his mother?

'She will be very happy, very very proud and very very humble knowing that a lot of people have bestowed their faith in her. She will dedicate everything she has and she has a lot to give. The one thing I would like to see more than anything else in the world is her standing on the steps of Number 10 in her own right!'

A 1950 picture, taken at a
Buckingham Palace garden
party

Arriving at the House of
Commons in 1959 as an
MP for the first time

Above: the Thatchers at home; *below:* the end of the 1978 Tory Party Conference in Brighton. On Mrs Thatcher's right is Conservative Party Chairman Lord Thorneycroft and on her left Dame Adelaide Doughty

8

Views

Paul Johnson – 'Most important of all, she is a Christian.'

Paul Johnson is a distinguished writer and well-respected political commentator. He became editor of *The New Statesman* in 1965 and remained in that office until 1970. His many publications include *A History of Christianity* and *Left of Centre*. In 1977 he announced his resignation from the Labour Party after twenty-four years of membership. His resignation statement appeared in *The New Statesman* entitled 'Farewell to the Labour Party', from which the following is an extract.

'When did it all begin to go wrong? I caught the first whiff of disaster in the Spring of 1969, when the Wilson Government and (as later events showed) Wilson himself were broken on the wheel of trade union power. The legislation foreshadowed in 'in place of strife' was unsatisfactory in a number of ways but it was plainly motivated by the laudable desire to curb the political and economic power of huge collective forces manipulated by small groups of men. As such its aim was libertarian and individualistic. The projected Bill was destroyed by a conspiracy of cynics, defeatists and trade union authoritarians inside and outside the cabinet which Wilson himself told me at the time "turned yellow" at the crucial point. It was no accident that the conspiracy was led by Jim Callaghan : his first decisive step on the road to Number Ten. No one to this day knows quite why Wilson resigned. But I suspect that disgust at the way things were going played a part in it. Wilson, with all his faults, once had liberal roots, a perky individualistic spirit of his own, and a genuine reluctance to see people pushed around. Lacking the will and the power to reverse the trend, he may have concluded that a collectivist party should be led by those who believe in authoritarianism and so made way for Callaghan – whose type Francis Bacon had in mind when he wrote, "Nothing doth more hurt in a state than that cunning men pass for wise."

'In the meantime the unions had been given the "closed shop" as part of the surrender. For me this was the turning point in my loyalty to the Party. For whatever the private reservations of certain cabinet ministers and backbenchers -- and some of them I know hate it as much as I do myself – they united without public dissent to legalise the closed shop. It became the Mark of Cain, blazed on the party's forehead. It was what the party now stood for : the right of union bureaucrats and bullyboys to coerce individuals into collective conformity as a prelude to further erosions of human freedom.

'Labour in Parliament is ceasing to be a party honourably organised to secure clearly defined public objectives. It is now a mere faction with office as its sole aim. In a system of belief where conscience is collectivised, there is no dependable barrier along the highway which ultimately leads to Auschwitz and Gulag.'

To state the obvious Paul Johnson is a man of enormous intellect but in no way does he epitomise the studious intellectual. He is a man of great charm, a ready wit and a strikingly infectious laugh. He recalled that his first meeting with Margaret Thatcher took place on the *Any Questions* programme shortly after she had been appointed as shadow minister of education replacing Edward Boyle who subsequently left the Conservative Party. He met her again at a party on the night of the 1970 election and by the time she had arrived, it was evident that the Conservatives had won.

'I saw her there and said, "Well you'll be in the Cabinet by the end of the week, you'll see." However, I noticed that she was still extremely nervous and doubtful as to whether or not she was going to make it, though it seemed perfectly obvious to me since she was by far the most formidable lady in the Tory Party. By then it was a fairly accepted convention that you must have at least one woman in the Cabinet and it was evident that she would be chosen – as indeed she was.

'She's very diffident you know in some ways and tends to underrate herself. There is an element of pessimism in her. Of course she has had to work very, very hard to get anywhere and there have been many setbacks in her life. She has never been able to take anything whatever for granted. There is none of this great expansiveness that feels yes, naturally I will be the leader of the party; yes naturally I will be Prime Minister: yes naturally I will succeed in this that and the other. She realises that anything she does accomplish will be only as the result of extreme concentration and the expenditure of a lot of energy and work and that even then an element of luck will be required.

'Whether she was a good Minister of Education, I don't know. I think she herself is inclined to be critical of her period there in that she accepted the conventional wisdom rather more readily than she should have done. The conventional wisdom in the sixties and early seventies on this as on other topics was that the more money you spent the better everything would be. That so long as the quantative element was there in all its profusion, then you were okay and would be running a good show. She now realises that equally if not more important, is the quality of the teachers and the actual curriculum. We should have concentrated on the essentials, namely the actual type of teacher, the type of teaching and what is taught. Those are the real basis of a good education system – it's not the millions and millions of pounds and the new schools.

'Accordingly, that is one lesson that I think she has learnt. And that in itself is very encouraging, because I've always thought that the hallmark of a good politician, particularly in this day and age when things move so fast, is the ability to learn from lessons. It's not the ability to avoid mistakes because everybody makes them. It's the ability to recognise the mistakes when you have made them and not to make them again and most importantly to learn from them. This in a curious way, although he was bad in other respects, was one of John F. Kennedy's great strengths. He did learn from his mistakes. Margaret does too. Of all the members of that 70/74 government, she is the one most critical of what it did. And it's all very well for people to say, "Well why didn't she say so at the time," but she was a fairly junior member of quite a high powered Cabinet. Quite often you may have grave reservations about what is being done by your colleagues but the nature of the Cabinet system is such now that you do tend to stick to your own departmental brief except on very special occasions.

'I used to say to Harold Wilson during his government, "Harold just find it in your heart, just for once, to say you've made a mistake. You'll find people will like you." He replied, "Yes I accept that Paul, I accept what you say, it's quite true. I will do that – but the trouble is I can't. I don't think I've made any!" Now Margaret isn't like that. She is self-critical, and that's right.

'Her great disadvantage throughout all her battles with her colleagues and in the House of Commons is that she hasn't been Prime Minister. She's almost the first Conservative party leader since Bonar Law to have become party leader without having previously been Prime Minister, or simultaneously. To lead a party in opposition when you haven't been Prime Minister, particularly if it's the Conservative Party is very difficult and adds to the already huge burden of being a woman.'

'How would you assess that burden and what particular form does it take both within the confines of Parliament and outside?'

'Well I think the burden is very considerable. A few years ago it would have been impossible because the Conservative party was male orientated in the sense that its activities were carried out within structures from which women were virtually banned. I'm referring to places like the Carlton Club or White's or Bucks, the essentially male precincts where Conservative policy took shape and found expression. The Clubs are still important to some extent and although they now have arrangements for women, she can't play a full part in that. Again there's a lot of the smoking room side of life in the House of Commons which women are excluded from. There are very few women in the House of Commons. It is very much a male place and the same applies to the House of Lords. Parliament is still essentially a male domain and it is undoubtedly difficult for a woman. Barbara Castle used to tell me about the difficulties she encountered being a woman in the Labour Party. In some ways it's even worse in that party because the hostility towards women among trade union MPs is very considerable. They tend to think that women shouldn't have official positions where they might be put in charge of men. Although it's true to say that the feeling isn't as strong as it used to be, it's still strong and one of the nastiest things that has been happening in the House of Commons is that Jim Callaghan, who also hates women getting to the top, tries to play on Margaret Thatcher being a woman during question time. He does this because he knows that there is a certain group of MPs just behind him in the House whom he can always get a cheap laugh out of if he makes a crack against her. But I don't think this upsets her any more. I think it probably did to begin with but she's had to be pretty tough and I think she's used to it now. But that's certainly one of the things she has had to contend with.

'Jim Callaghan doesn't like women getting to the top; he likes them in the home but he doesn't like formidable women like Mrs Thatcher. Although in theory, it's perfectly true that the Labour Party believe in the total equality of women, in many ways they are more opposed and less progressive towards women than the Tories. Accordingly, it may be that it was easier for Mrs Thatcher to become leader of her party than it would have been had she been Labour.'

It's always a considerable dilemma for any party to elect a new leader. Each of the candidates have different qualities and people have varying views as to the essential attributes of a good leader. But what particular strength or quality did Margaret Thatcher possess which set her apart and resulted in her ultimately being chosen as leader?

'I think it was one quite simple reason – her great courage. There was dissatisfaction with Heath. There was no obvious successor. The people who might have stood as successors were afraid to do so and didn't. Margaret Thatcher was the only one who had the courage to stand and that's why she won, in the long run there are always a sufficient number of Conservative MPs who respect courage. They rate that pretty highly, and rightly so in my view because it's the most important of all political virtues. She has the guts to lead the party. Even her most venomous opponents will admit that she has bounteous reserves of truly Churchillian valour!'

'As a highly experienced political commentator and a close observer of many of the country's leading politicians over a span of some twenty years, how would you define Margaret Thatcher's foremost characteristics both as a politician and as a person?'

'There are many things I like about her which might not appeal to others. First of all and most important of all, she is a Christian. She is the first proper Christian as a political leader that we've had for a very long time! I wouldn't care to say how far back you would have to go to find another. She is what you might call an orthodox Christian in the sense that she accepts the teachings of her church and is not a kind of subversive, trendy revolutionary element in it. She *does* believe in the ten commandments. She *does* make very clear distinctions in her mind between what is morally right and wrong. One of the points she continually makes, and is gradually getting across, is that it used to be thought that the Labour Party had morals on its side, that it somehow had a respect for equality, justice and moral goodness which the Conservatives, the party of capital, didn't possess, but that now the pendulum has swung the other way. Today it is the Conservatives who

70

stand for certain moral absolutes which Labour no longer stands for. There are now very few Christians in the higher reaches of the Labour Party. But whilst the Conservative Party is no longer the great sort of Anglican Party it used to be, there is still a very strong Church element in it which she represents and speaks for. She says and fervently believes that the Conservative Party is there to uphold certain absolute moral standards such as it's wrong to steal; it's wrong to kill; ordinary ten commandment stuff. She says this with complete passionate intensity and conviction and I think it evokes a very definite response among ordinary people – not the sort you meet at West End dinner parties – but ordinary people throughout the country. They like to hear someone at the top of public life speak out for these ordinary things that they were brought up on and regret seeing disappear in our rapidly changing society, and Margaret's youth was based on strict adherence to all the Christian values.

'Secondly, she is a very intelligent and enlightened person. She is a good listener and is actually interested in ideas. If you read her speeches, you may not agree with them but they are all actually on themes. She does discuss general philosophical and political ideas : she isn't dogmatic or self-opinionated. There's always meat in her speeches. A speech by Jim, if you actually begin to look at it carefully, falls apart. There's nothing in it, just politician's verbiage – in actual fact that is usually true of most politicians. Enoch Powell is an exception. He always has an argument, a theme, something which appeals to the mind, whether or not you agree with it. To some extent Margaret is like that.

'Thirdly, she has a tremendous amount of energy. I always admire people like that. Undoubtedly it's a very necessary qualification for a politician and she has more than most. Politicians are curious in that they rise to events. The adrenalin flows and they somehow find reserves of energy even when they are tired. But she's in training all the time and seems to lead a very healthy life – she's very fit. Right at the end of a very hard day, after she's had a long committee meeting, she starts tidying everything up –

the cushions are rearranged and the furniture is straightened, and so on. There's a sort of irrepressible housewife in her!

'Fourthly, one of her shining qualities is her honesty. So far as I have been able to see in my dealings with her, she is absolutely straight and I think that's terribly important. For that reason it will be nice to have Mrs Thatcher as Prime Minister. There is something rather compellingly direct about her. A prominent member of the Royal Family said, a few weeks ago, "You know, I like that Mrs Thatcher, she always looks you straight in the eye." It's a curious thing but apparently people are shy and hardly ever look Royalty in the eye. Margaret does. She looks at everyone straight in the eye.

'She is a good mixer who genuinely likes and sympathises with her fellow human beings. She may not be very popular among the upper middle class but many working class women think a great deal of her. They know she was born above a grocer's shop. They know that she has had to fight every inch of the way in a man's world. They know she has got to the top through sheer determination, hard work, courage and brains. This is important because working-class women no longer do what their husbands tell them. In the old days of canvassing, the lady of the house would come to the door and I'd say, "Are you going to vote Labour?" – "I'll have to ask Dad," came the reply. Then in a couple of minutes she'd come back and say, all right we're voting Labour. Of course that still exists but very much less than it used to.' Margaret Thatcher knows what a shopping basket is – she has never lost her motherly instinct. She is constantly fussing around wondering whether you're too hot, too cold, or getting enough to eat.

'Margaret Thatcher for the reasons which you have described has had to surmount unprecedented obstacles. She is a trailblazer who has laid the way open for other women to follow in her path. If she became Prime Minister, what problems would she have to face and would she adopt a different approach to her predecessors?'

'This is the key question. She is a Conservative and the

Conservative Party is meant to conserve. It's not meant to go round turning things upside down as it did in 1970/74. I know that she doesn't want to get involved in a lot of legislation. In fact what she really wants to do is to pull the Government out of a lot of operations which it's engaged in at the moment. She believes that there is just too much government, too many laws, too many civil servants. And I think there's growing agreement over this, not just among the Conservatives. She doesn't want to have a radical programme of change but she does want radical approaches, that is away from the prevailing wisdom of the sixties and seventies which has proved so disastrous for this country. To strike the right balance between those changes which are absolutely necessary and change just for its own sake is always a difficult problem.'

'Would the Unions pose a threat to her premiership?'

'I don't think she'll have much difficulty with the Trade Unions. This is a complete myth. The Trade Unions are not in a fighting mood. They are afraid of inflation like everyone else. They are afraid of unemployment like everyone else. They're not going to pick a purely political row because they know they wouldn't get away with it – after all that would be more or less saying to the country we're a one party state, we are only going to have a party that agrees with us and they can't say that. Their members won't back them if they do. So that is not the problem. Most trade union leaders are realists. They do not want a confrontation unless it is forced upon them and you may be sure that Margaret Thatcher has absolutely no intention of doing that. She is not a rash woman. She is not quick tempered, unlike her predecessor. She is a conciliator who would infinitely prefer to solve problems on an amicable basis. She doesn't want confrontation and is always prepared to listen to the other party's point of view. So I repeat that is not a problem.

'I think there *will* be problems with certain interest groups in Britain that are militant and violent and will not accept the dictate of the ballot box – the left wing of the Labour Party and some of these fringe groups do preach

73

violence quite openly now. But frankly, I don't think that will amount to very much. She may also have a certain amount of trouble within the Tory Party itself because here she is faced with a dilemma. Does she create a Government leaving out the rather discontented elements? Does she exclude those and have a government of people who are completely backing her, but with the possibility of a discontented movement building up if anything goes wrong as it inevitably does in any government from time to time, or does she try and include them all? I used to say to Harold Wilson who never took my advice on this, never reward your enemies. It's always a mistake in politics to reward your enemies, because they will take this as an invitation to do something even nastier to you. But it's something that Harold always did. I think Margaret ought to draw a distinction between those of her critics who have actually behaved reasonably well, as some of them have, and those who are openly hostile. But she's a tolerant woman you know, she hasn't got this bitter side to her nature of being unable to forgive injuries as some politicians have. She would be willing to include the whole bloody lot provided they didn't impose impossible conditions and provided there was a reasonable understanding that they were going to behave themselves.'

People in this country seem to be drifting along without any real conviction, without any apparent goal in sight. There appears to be a feeling of apathy and an atmosphere of general disincentive. What effect or impact, I asked, would Margaret Thatcher have on the mood of the country as PM?

'I think she will provide a fresh start! She is a woman of very great strength of character and very clear ideas who will provide precisely the leadership the country needs. She has a straightforward consistent philosophy which she preaches in all its simplicity and with complete honesty. She does believe that hard work must be rewarded, that intelligence must be recognised and encouraged and that incentives must be restored.

'The real term to use about her is "expert". She is the

first party leader for many years who has a thorough grasp of public finance and who knows how taxation policies, Government expenditure and economic performance intermesh. One of the chief reasons why Britain prospered in the 19th century was that such Prime Ministers as William Pitt, Robert Peel and Gladstone personally understood every aspect of public finance and were on the whole better informed than even their ablest Treasury and Board of Trade officials. Margaret Thatcher, as anyone who has heard her give off-the-cuff answers to complex financial questions will acknowledge, is a return to this invaluable tradition.

'She will provide a moral leadership. Of course no government can say, "We'll come in and abolish crime," but what people would like to see is a government which actually says and means that it intends to do its level best to tackle the criminal elements in our society – unlike the Labour Party who in many cases have backed up law breakers, whether at Grunwick or in other areas.

'She wholeheartedly believes in Law and Order. She is a woman of her word. Once she actually gets into No. 10 she is going to be a very, very big success. A fresh start is precisely what she will provide and that is the whole point.'

Brian Walden – 'There is no one in politics I would sooner trust.'

Brian Walden joined the Labour Party in 1951 at the age of nineteen. He entered Parliament as MP for Birmingham All Saints in 1964 and remained in that constituency for ten years. Then in 1974 he represented Birmingham Ladywood. In 1977, he gave up his seat and succeeded Peter Jay as presenter for ITV's *Weekend World*.

He was brought up strictly in a working class mining family and instilled with primitive beliefs. Indeed his mother was subjugated to such an extent that she was never even allowed to eat in the same room as his father. Throughout her life she was forced to eat in the kitchen and was totally forbidden, at risk of physical violence, to express an opinion on anything at all. He was taught what he describes as the Midland and Northern working class view of the role of women in society : they were useful in two rooms of the house, the kitchen and the bedroom, and they spent their time there.

Parliament too has its fair share of residual male chauvinism and when Brian Walden first met Margaret Thatcher, one of the few female residents of that essentially male dominated world, his impressions were not exactly favourable.

'I didn't like her at first, not at all, but I couldn't have been more wrong. First impressions aren't always the best and in this case the reverse proved to be true. In fact I happened to mention that I disliked her to a friend of mine, a fellow Labour MP and he told me I had totally misjudged her. Of course I didn't just accept his view but I naturally looked at her with slightly different eyes and soon began to realise how wrong I had been.'

'What particular facets of her nature invoked this change of mind?'

'She is entirely trustworthy! I would put that at the top of the list. There is no one in politics I would sooner trust than Margaret! I would trust her with any confidence. She would never betray it even if it was very much against her own interests not to do so! She is a very warm, friendly, decent person. She isn't a snob – she really isn't. I know that traditionally by all appearances, she ought to be and I also know that successful people of lower class origin are often the worst snobs because they are insecure. For some reason, she isn't insecure and she isn't a snob. I really don't think it makes much difference to her who she is talking to. She has as much or as little interest in Dukes as in housewives. There is no element of the English vice which is disliking people not for what they are but for what they seem to be. There is no element of that in her at all. She is a compassionate person and people speak extremely well of her in that sphere. For instance, if you will not allow a man to assist you and do things for you which he ought to be doing because his marriage is breaking up and you don't want him to be worried, what would you call that? I call it compassion. I have heard several stories of a similar kind where Margaret has gone out of her way to say to people, "Don't bother so and so because he has difficult marital problems."

'People respect that side of her nature, it's a very feminine side. It would never even cross Jim Callaghan's mind not to bother somebody because his marriage was breaking up, it might interestingly enough have crossed Harold Wilson's because he was a very kind man in private whatever may have been his public failings. Margaret is a very sympathetic person and can comfort people and calm them down if they're very distressed, but she doesn't have the simple foolish kind of tolerance which is destroying some of the best things in our society. I haven't any compassion either for people who beat up old ladies with lead pipes in back alleys. I don't wish to hear about their deprived backgrounds. I remember my generation in the thirties. My father never worked until the war started. We were just as deprived as they were. I'm not an exponent of what I would call collective compassion which has gone to ridiculous lengths and in so far as she is tough about that she's right because some of these young men need bringing up sharp. But yes, she does have a great deal of individual compassion. Women are more compassionate because in some ways they are more imaginative than men and I think she's like that – very much so! Margaret retains her personal kindness, her essential femininity, whilst doing a very difficult job. If she were Prime Minister, it would be easier but doing it as the critic, as the Leader of the Opposition, which is a fault finding role, that is a remarkable achievement and I think it is only part of a series of linked achievements.'

In 1928 women attained voting parity with men but who would have envisaged even the remotest possibility of seeing a woman at the helm of a major party only fifty years later. Not even the most romantic visionary could have foretold such a reversal of historical tradition. But why Margaret Thatcher? What special or unusual qualities does she possess? Why did destiny choose her?

'One of her most striking qualities is her fantastic, unbelievable diligence. She has an amazing capacity for work. She is not a genius, she is not staggeringly brilliant but I have never known anybody with a better capacity for devoting themselves single-mindedly to mastering something. I suppose this may in part be due to her legal training. If you are a tax barrister, your job is to master complex details. But she has a uniquely well developed gift for it. I've never known anyone with quite as much aptitude for mastering detail and it is the key and the secret to her achievements. She gave Denis Healey a tremendous hammering in an economic debate just before the Tory leadership election and I always think that probably swung the election for her. She took the pants off Healey and that's not easy to do but she did it by mastering detail, not by brilliant oratory, she's not a brilliant speaker but she can command fact. Anything that can be done by effort Margaret can do.

'Her second impressive quality is her tremendous determination. She must have an iron will though it doesn't really show itself because she's a very kind, friendly, cheerful person unless attacked, and after all which of us are kindly, friendly and cheerful when attacked. But if treated decently, she's an easy going, goodhearted woman with a great sense of purpose.

'Her third great attribute might rather surprise you. I think she typifies majority feeling in this country. She has a grip on people's imagination because their beliefs are very much like her beliefs. She enshrines the majority view. That's a great strength for her, a very great strength, especially as she is wholly sincere. She hasn't just worked these opinions out because she has decided that they represent the majority view, as some people in politics do. I instance the Prime Minister as one example who determines quite coldly what the majority think and then chooses to pretend to believe it or perhaps in time actually comes to believe it. Margaret isn't like that at all. She instinctively believes it, so she is sincere and the sincerity shows.

'Her fourth great strength or quality is her resilience. She's had some nasty blows and she doesn't always win. She is not a first class orator and some of the people she is up against are so she takes a beating from time to time. But she is very resilient. She has a tremendous capacity to come back and to keep coming back. She is a born fighter – a warrior. The wounds heal quickly or at least appear to, but perhaps she has the capacity to turn them in upon herself and not show them. I think she has had to learn to live without sharing many confidences – that builds up a kind of discipline. I suspect that maybe she does bleed a lot; she haemorrhages internally but it never shows and she has the capacity to come back and try again, largely successfully.

'I think it is a remarkable achievement for a woman to become leader of the Conservative Party. That Party is not normally led in Opposition by people who haven't been Prime Minister, and to be a woman as well – there's never been anything like it in British politics – ever! She's never had any great connections in the Tory Party or belonged to any of their particular establishments, nor had help from any great patrons. She's never *had* any great patrons. But that's only part of the story. Added to that is the enormous difficulty of *being a woman*, which is considerable and you have to admire the way she has carried that burden.'

'Having analysed her predominant characteristics and some of the reasons which were contributory factors in her ultimate succession to the leadership, how would you assess her performance after three years in the role as leading lady?'

'It was predicted that she would be awful and be eaten

79

alive by all these experienced old pros and Callaghan is an experienced old pro. He certainly had every intention of eating her alive if he could. I don't think he has. I think she has had a rather remarkable success in the House. I think she's amazingly imaginative. She's the only Tory leader I've known who has grasped the fact that the Party image has changed and that today it's a people's party. She knows that you can support a football team, like fish and chips and tomato sauce on everything and still be a Tory voter. She's adopted an imaginative approach and that says volumes for her courage. Remember, it's easy to adopt an imaginative approach if you're Harold Macmillan, married to a Devonshire, a close associate of Winston's. If you're in the inner circle and accepted as the top of the top, it's very easy to say, "Come on fellas, we must be bold, we must be imaginative." But if you're the grocer's daughter, with no connections, who has done it all by ability and sheer hard work, to then call for a new approach, that's very hard indeed!

'Her imagination and insight as a Tory leader is remarkable and her views help her because they are very close to those of most of the population. She's never drifted away from the basic realities of life. She mixes easily with people and when she learns to swear in public, she will be even better.'

'Where do her weaknesses lie?'

'Her weaknesses lie in the spheres of trust. I think she's too trusting. She could do with being marginally more suspicious.'

'How does she compare with past leaders of the Opposition?'

'She is the best Tory leader of the Opposition I have ever seen since I entered Parliament in 1964. I have been told by those who saw him during the post-war period that there was a remarkable quality about Winston that nobody could duplicate. Though in some ways he was a very bad leader of the Opposition, in other ways, because he was probably the greatest Englishman who has ever lived, there was a kind of aura about him. Remember the Tories

80

were in Government for a very long time, so apart from Winston, they haven't had any leaders in Opposition except those that I've seen since the war, namely Home, Heath and Margaret and she is much the best.

'She does her homework better. She understands the House better – she knows when to be silent. One of the difficulties about leading the Opposition is a rather over-whelming desire to talk all the time. She doesn't. She has a better instinct for the jugular than Ted. Alec had none at all, his appeal was quite different, his appeal was that of the calm statesman, which in fact he was, but that doesn't necessarily make you a good leader of the Opposition. I think Ted wanted the jugular but he could never find it. She can; she can draw blood. She knows where the weak-nesses are and she probes for them and every so often, more often than not she hits them. She can annoy the Prime Minister and that takes some doing because he deliberately doesn't want to be annoyed. It's part of his pose not to be annoyed, because he's above all such normal emotions. After all, he has the world to run doesn't he and therefore he doesn't want to appear petty. He likes to patronise her. But she's got through the shield on more than one occasion. I think she's a very good Leader of the Opposition, very good indeed!'

Prime Ministers question time has tended to confuse the public rather than enlighten them. It hasn't exactly inspired confidence in the inner workings of the House. That's not very surprising because the initial impact is to say the least rather bewildering. It may be called question time but a fair proportion of the inmates are quite deter-mined not to hear the question. There is a considerable amount of barracking and jeering and a plentiful supply of "oos" and "aahs". For some the fifteen-minute session seems to provide a heaven-sent opportunity to relieve all those pent up frustrations, all those burning hatreds and, if their timing is right, there is the added bonus of getting a laugh at the target's expense. When Mrs Thatcher rises to question the PM she is heralded by a cacophony of sound, and some eloquent slogans such as "that bloody woman" and "ditch the bitch"! How difficult is that to contend with or is it all part of the contest?

'This woman can take anything – anything! I don't know whether like Sir Walter Scott's Knight of Old, she may eventually die from the internal wounds – I don't know whether that might happen, I suspect not, but I repeat this woman can take anything and these people only cheapen themselves. I don't think they really do her any harm. After the initial shock of realising that people can abuse you in such a way, I think she has learnt to live with it. For a sensible man to get up and score a palpable hit using decent, sensible language, that worries people. Although members of Parliament pretend to have no kind of objectivity at all when they are sitting in the House, they actually do. They know when their side is winning and when it's losing, but a barrage of cheap abuse, I don't think that worries Margaret greatly. Anyway, she is far tougher than they are and has done far more with her life than they have ever done with theirs and she probably treats it with the contempt it deserves – she probably despises it. Not all the Left are as bad as that but some of them are barbarians. However as is always the case with any foul blow in life, even if it's sport, it demeans the person who commits the foul rather than the person who is fouled! Increasingly in the last ten years, to my deep regret, the left now fights dirty. To put it in footballing terms, they kick you before the match starts – the first tackle is a foul. It has something to do with the changes in our society which make this kind of conduct more permissable and acceptable than it used to be. But Margaret takes it calmly and with dignity.'

'*Would* you describe her as a dignified person?'

'Yes, she has a great deal of dignity – almost too much. I would prefer her to loosen a bit but she certainly doesn't lack dignity.'

Margaret Thatcher's image has attracted a great deal of comment. To some extent it's explicable on the grounds that she's a woman – after all you never hear people commenting on Jim Callaghan's well cut suits or passing remarks as to whether or not he has changed his hair style. But there is a feeling among some people on both sides of the House that her public image is different from her private one. Politicians depend to an ever increasing extent on the media.

'Emphasising your word "loosen", should Margaret Thatcher adopt a more relaxed approach to the television interview?'

'I don't think she has great media problems but yes she's too tight. She isn't sufficiently spontaneous. If she would speak on camera the way she talks off camera it would be better, but I stress I don't think she does it badly by any means. However, she could do it better, she does need more spontaneity, less suffering of fools, the occasional cuss word, and broader smiles. When she really wants to laugh, she should laugh. After all Winston used to spend his whole time laughing and crying in about equal proportions. Yes, she should loosen a bit but having said that, one's got to be fair. What more do you want this woman to do. She's carrying several crosses already. To say, do all that and relax and be yourself, these are the standards of absolute perfection! But, by the standards of absolute perfection, she could be more spontaneous.

'Her public image *is* still a bit starchy. I think she is respected and regarded as being quite capable of being Prime Minister but I think people still feel that she's a bit of a blue stocking, a bit unspontaneous. Her image problem is that she is insufficiently relaxed. However it's worth pointing out that she has had some fairly rough brutal treatment and that can't have helped her. The media is in general left wing, that's no secret. It's like saying the City is right wing, what would you expect. A lot of interviewers are not interested in getting anything out of her, they are interested in bringing her down. They want to show that they know more about it than she does – fat chance, but they conduct the interviews accordingly. This quite naturally tends to freeze her further and she hasn't yet learnt to grin under hostile criticism and to turn it back against the interviewer. But that's a very rare art and

83

you can't really blame her for it. It would help her to smile. It would help her to learn how to cope with the interviewer who plainly doesn't intend to be fair, who is there not to listen to what she has to say, but to make a series of points for himself. There are such people. She resorts to exactly what you would expect her to resort to – facts. That often isn't the best way. Often the best way is to smile and say, "Dear, dear, you really are in a bad mood this evening, aren't you." She hasn't quite learned to do that yet. She will. She's a Truman figure. It wasn't until he became President of the United States that people realised what a great man he was. Now they eulogise about him in the history books, quite rightly so in my view. He had a capacity for growth. She does too. She can grow into any job you give her, including the Premiership.'

In recent years, people have become somewhat indifferent, somewhat apathetic in their attitude towards politics and politicians. The oft heard criticism is that there isn't really any major difference between the two main parties – but is there?

'Does Margaret Thatcher offer the country a real choice or to use Paul Johnson's words a fresh start?'

'There wasn't any particular difference between the Government of 1970 and 1974 or the previous Government or the subsequent Government. But Margaret Thatcher is a defender of a liberal society. She believes in all the classic verities of English liberty. She doesn't want the State to play an ever increasing role. After all, the State is the least efficient of all our great institutions. We do need less government. I don't like the State playing its present part. I think that ordinary people, particularly within the family, are perfectly capable, indeed much more capable of making their own decisions than the State.

'The most vital issue in British politics today is whether we really exist to serve the State or whether the State exists to serve us! I've no doubt what her view is. Her view is that the State is a useful tool that must have certain regular functions, that we can't go back to the 19th century, but that it's all gone too far, much, much too far. She does offer a choice to the people of this country. I have the highest hopes of her there because I am quite certain that she believes it. She articulates genuinely felt beliefs. That's why she does it so effectively. It hasn't been devised to win votes, in some ways it loses votes because people are always frightened to change from what they have. A lot of people are afraid to take the chance. But if the chance is not taken, then the issue will be settled and we shall essentially exist to serve the State. Anything you choose to do that the State doesn't like, the State will stop you from doing, with or without justice.'

'If Britain leads the way as it has done so many times in the past and becomes the first country in Western Europe to elect a female Prime Minister, how would you envisage her chances of success?'

'I think she would be one of the best Prime Ministers this country has seen – one of the best. Certainly by post-war standards, after all, who would she be competing against? I suppose her competition would be Macmillan who she likes and enormously respects. He was a great post-war PM but I think she could excel him because she's got more to do than he had. If we are really to see the Britain she wants, she has an enormous amount to salvage. I think she is capable of it. Her own instincts are her own best guide. She's at her best when she follows her own instincts. She has a fine set of brains, a good head and an enormous amount of common sense. She's a woman of great feeling. I only wish she wouldn't suppress it so much. She is a very passionate woman. She tends to hold that side of her nature in a tight rein, in too tight a rein in my view. I wouldn't mind some of the passion burning forth a bit. She has a passionate heart, she should let that flair forward occasionally.

'She is not in the least offended by criticism, provided the criticisms are well motivated, not abuse. She listens to what she is told. If she is told, "Look, this isn't quite right Margaret," she doesn't say, "Leave the room, I never want to speak to you again," she has no foolish vanity of that kind. She listens and tries. She possesses those qualities which as a nation we have increasingly come to lack, energy, discipline and dedication.

'She frightens the left – the left in general. No Tory leader in my time has been more straightforward in their condemnation of Marxism. It's not pre-election guff just to work everybody up. She doesn't intend that things should go on as before. She doesn't want the State to play an ever increasing role. You can understand why the Socialists don't like that because what they are really worried about is that it will prove to be popular. That once people actually see it in motion, they'll say, "We actually prefer this to what we had before." That's why she is such a great threat to the Labour Party. Not everything she wants is possible. That's not a criticism of her, it's true of all Oppositions because they are shut off from the vital pieces of information which they only see when they become the Government. Not all of what she wants to do could be done, but seventy-five per cent of it could and she'll do it. She doesn't believe that the State should dominate everything. She doesn't believe that there has to be huge personal taxation. She doesn't believe that there's got to be vast bureaucracy. She doesn't believe that the State has got to be involved in whole areas of national life which it has no business in anyway. She doesn't believe it and she'll change it! If that's what the British people want, and I suspect they do, then this woman is going to give it to them. This woman means what she says, it's as simple as that. That is what makes her the most exciting figure in British politics. She is totally honest! That's a frightening thing to be in politics, wholly honest – it's most unusual.

'Of course it's normally regarded, falsely in my view, as a great political asset to be able to dissemble, to be able to keep things secret, to hide under false appearances. Franklyn Roosevelt did it and Abraham Lincoln did it. But for a Party leader not to dissemble, not to want to disguise the facts, that's almost unique. The amount of dissembling she does is miniscule, she will cover the occasional erring colleague, that's about the extent of it. She tends to say exactly what she thinks and that's her greatest appeal. It is also the reason for the hostility. There's no element of deception in her character. That's quite remarkable!

'She would be an outstanding Prime Minister, I guess. I think this country needs her too. I think this country needs someone like Margaret Thatcher, at least for a time. If she wins the next election, if the British people give her a chance, it will be the first piece of luck she has ever had in her life for Margaret is a stranger to luck. If she wins, it will be the most romantic happening in British politics since Disraeli became Prime Minister, indeed it will exceed it. In years to come great novels and poems will be written about her. She will do more for the advance of women than all the acts of Parliament and all the events of history – she will truly liberate them. She deserves to win. I've never known anybody who deserves to win more. I know you don't always get your just deserts – that's reserved for Heaven.'

Lord Shinwell – 'Ladies have an advantage.'

Lord Emanuel Shinwell, Baron of Easington Durham was born in London in 1884. He was one of eleven children and was raised in Glasgow of a poor Jewish immigrant family. He was the Labour MP for Linlithgow from 1922–1924 and from 1928–1931. He then represented the Seaham Division of Durham from 1935–1950 and the Easington Division of Durham from 1950–70. During his exceptionally long lifetime in politics, he has held many prestige offices. He was Parliamentary Secretary to the Department of Mines, Financial Secretary to the War Office, Minister of Fuel and Power, Secretary of State for War and Minister of Defence. As a boxing fan, his pugilistic exploits have even been seen on the floor of The House of Commons. He is also reputed to have a fiery temper which is in itself tempered by a sharp turn of wit.

Lord Shinwell and playwright Ben Travers made an outstanding double act on Mike Parkinson's BBC television chat show. It was on that show that Shinwell had this to say about Margaret Thatcher: 'You've got to be fair to your political opponents. I'm even fair to Maggie. She's a nice woman, a very nice woman!'

Lord Manny Shinwell seemed somewhat surprised that I had come to talk to him about Margaret Thatcher. 'You should talk to someone in her own Party,' he said. However, he soon relented when I explained that I was anxious to canvass all shades of opinion. Having had several conversations with her over the years, he described her as a warm, friendly, approachable person who he laughingly observed is quite naturally very critical of the Labour Party. 'If she said anything complimentary about the Labour Party, they would sue her for libel.' Speaking of her approachability, he finds that she is more approachable than many would-be Prime Ministers have been and indeed are. She is whole-hearted in her views, means exactly what she says and is undoubtedly anxious to promote reforms: though precisely what shape these reforms will take Lord Shinwell finds somewhat ambiguous. As to her beliefs, he said that although she holds strong Tory views, her outlook is probably more radical than she gets credit for. He felt that this lack of recognition for her radical approach may in some way be due to her origin. 'If one's origin is lower middle class, one's views are to some extent conditioned by that. If her origin had been aristocratic, she would act differently; she would be more inflexible.' Enlarging on this viewpoint, he explained that if she had been the daughter of a landowner with aristocratic ancestors that would have conditioned her attitude in society. Being the daughter of a grocer – and Lord Shinwell was at pains to stress that he had nothing whatsoever against grocers – meant that the way she was brought up in terms of outlook and patterns of behaviour were inevitably different.

Setting aside for a moment the attitudes which may or may not be symptomatic of a particular background, Lord Shinwell turned his attention towards the female species. 'All women,' he said with a wry smile, 'have certain advantages over their rather sensitive male counterpart. Being a woman undoubtedly gives Margaret Thatcher a definite advantage. For although it is said that women generally dislike the idea of having a woman as Prime Minister, I don't believe that this is fundamentally true. I think the fact that she's a woman will probably result in her attracting more votes from her own sex.'

Lord Shinwell then paused for a moment to reflect upon the distinction between the present leader of the Conservative Party and her predecessor. He went on, 'There is a vast difference between Thatcher and Heath. I wouldn't ever impugn Heath's integrity, but his defect, and it's an obvious one to those who have watched him, is his reliability on an idea. Once he has presented it, he won't let go. Thatcher isn't remotely like that. She is very flexible in the political sphere and in that respect she is a much better leader than Ted Heath. A good leader must be ready to compromise.' But what about the Premiership itself? I posed the obvious question. Would Margaret Thatcher make a good Prime Minister? 'If she's got the backing of the general public and if the Party remains loyal to her and set aside their feelings of envy, particularly those who are left out of office, then she should be a success.' He surmised that she had invoked envy simply because she was seeking to achieve those goals that others felt were within their own capabilities. 'There is no limit to the belief that politicians have in their own ability,' he observed sardonically. He then remarked that he would rather not make any comparisons between her and Labour lady politicians since people were inclined to get jealous.

No conversation with Lord Shinwell would be complete without some reference to the Labour Party and I asked him whether the Party had changed over the past few years. He answered in this way. 'The Labour Party has become more academic. I am not criticising people with academic training but they seem to create the impression that they are more interested in their own personal ambition than in getting the country on its feet. I would never leave the Labour Party but I criticise it when necessary. I refrain from criticism sometimes because I don't want to destroy them.'

Finally I asked Lord Shinwell whether he thought that Margaret Thatcher was the best choice as leader of the Tory Party. He seemed to enjoy the question. 'Although the Tory Party undoubtedly has a lot of talent, the Party are not throwing up many people out of which you could pick a potential Prime Minister.' He explained that whilst he didn't deny their talent, it certainly existed, it was one thing to have talent and another thing to have the capacity to lead and gain the respect of the electorate. In that sphere he contended, she didn't have much competition. 'She is a very astute politician, has the courage of her convictions and has proved to be a good mixer with the general public.

'As I've already said,' laughed Lord Shinwell, 'the ladies have an advantage. I should know, I've had three wives!'

Lord Pannell – 'She was the only one man enough to stand for the leadership.'

'I am writing a book about Margaret Thatcher.' 'So!' 'I understand you were her pair* for fifteen years.' 'So what!' 'Well I'm sure you came to know her very well during that period.' An awkward silence permeated the telephone line, somebody had to speak. 'I would be very grateful if you

*A pair comprises two MPs from opposing parties who agree not to vote on a specific issue during an agreed space of time.

could spare half an hour of your time to talk about her.' 'Four o'clock Tuesday, House of Lords,' came the reply. Not a very auspicious beginning but at least there was hope.

Tuesday arrived and Lord Pannell greeted me without any trace of the hostility which I had experienced on the telephone. Like many people, he possibly has a natural distrust of that particular instrument. Lord Pannell, who is a very amiable, friendly and forthright person, first came into the House of Commons in 1949 as Labour MP for West Leeds. He specialised in the history and procedure of the House, took a leading part in women's causes, held office as Minister of Works and entered the House of Lords in 1974. His first meeting with Margaret Thatcher (then Margaret Roberts) took place in Dartford in 1950. This was the scene of her first political fight and Charles Pannell was Chairman of the Dartford Division of the Labour Party and leader of the Erith council. 'She was a young up and coming politician and was easily the most effective Conservative candidate that we had ever had in the Dartford Division. She fought the seat both in 1950 and 1951 and although at the time she was an industrial chemist with Joe Lyons, she took digs in the constituency and worked it extremely hard. In fact she always worked it as if she meant to win it though there was never the slightest chance because Labour had a majority of 20,000 in 1945. Norman Dodds, who was the sitting Labour MP, was a very considerable man indeed. He had a great deal of regard for her, and Margaret remained on very good terms with the Labour Party whilst she was the candidate. She was always easy in conversation and in those days she was *known* as Margaret. A look of disgust appeared on Lord Pannell's face as he contemplated her new styled christian name. 'I rather deplore the use of the name Maggie. Margaret suits her as a person because she has plenty of dignity. Maggie is a sort of slumming term and I don't like it very much at all. She should never have allowed the newspapers to have called her by that name. She should have made it abundantly clear from the start that she wanted to be known as Margaret.

'In 1955 she stayed away because she had twins – one better than average – and in 1959 when she entered Parliament, she came in rather the mood to teach the House how it should go on and in her maiden speech put forward a proposal to admit the press into local authority meetings.' At that time Charles Pannell, by now an experienced parliamentarian, advised Margaret Thatcher that it would be wise for her to have a regular pair since she was anxious to spend a good deal of time in her London constituency. He became her pair in 1959 and the arrangement continued until his entry into the House of Lords. 'I want to say this. During all that time she was what I would call a very fastidious pair. By fastidious, I mean that she would never have thought of breaking a pair. She always stood by her word. She is a very honourable and straightforward person and I had no complaint during those fifteen years.'

Of course Margaret Thatcher has come a long way since those far off days of 1959 and Lord Pannell reflected upon the now famous leadership battle of 1975. 'I never understood what the grievances were with Heath who was a very considerable man but there was obviously a brooding discontent with him among his own Party who felt compelled to hold an election. As an intelligent observer on the other side, who knows more about this place than most, I feel sure that Heath was pretty confident that he was going to emerge as the victor.' He attributes Margaret Thatcher's victory to the undisputed fact that she had the redoubtable courage to jump in at the deep end. 'When the chips were down, she was the only one man enough in the Conservative Party to stand for the leadership.' Whilst Lord Pannell didn't comment on the result of this particular election he gave his judgement of the lady who sits at the helm of the Tory Party today. 'I have no doubt that she is the best leader now because she brings a definitive sense of purpose and a certain hardness to the party. This has been particularly evident in her stand on immigration, a stand which as a life long Labour member, I totally oppose.'

Over a period of some twenty-eight years, the two

parties not surprisingly came to know each other very well. They enjoyed a sense of humour of the kind which develops between two people who understand each other and they shared many an 'in' joke about people in the House. This reference to friendship reminded Lord Pannell of a newspaper article profiling Margaret Thatcher in which she had said that she could always rely on her pair who was a personal friend. This brought an immediate and angry response from some of his party members. 'One or two irate left wingers actually wrote to me saying, "How dare you consort with the enemy?" My secretary, who saw the correspondence, asked if she could reply to it and then merely thanked the people concerned for their letters and promised to pass them on to me as soon as it was convenient. I have never found Margaret unfriendly in any way and one of the odd things I can't quite reconcile myself to is the fact that she has always been on good terms with members of the Labour Party in the tea room. There has never been any of that sharp hostility which people tend to build up.'

Finally, the prospect of having a female Prime Minister and the inevitable question of whether or not she would make a success of the job was raised. Whilst Lord Pannell refused to believe in anything other than a clear Labour victory at the next election, he reluctantly agreed to make a supreme effort and steal himself just for a moment to contemplate the possibility of a moment in history being made and the electorate choosing a woman as leader of the country. 'It's difficult for me to judge whether or not she would be a good Prime Minister because we have never had an animal quite like her before. However, she is certainly a very professional and honourable politician. But I am not in the House of Commons now and haven't worked closely enough with her to know whether or not she is a good delegator — an important hallmark of any Prime Minister. I would however like to say this. I always knew where she stood. She is a very honest person and if I could sum her up in one sentence, I would say she'd make a good friend.'

Harold Wilson – 'I've no doubt at all that Margaret was elected because of her courage.'

The Right Honourable Sir (James) Harold Wilson Labour MP for the Ormskirk Division of Lancashire 1945–50 and for Huyton since 1950. He was President of the Board of Trade from 1947 till he resigned in 1951. In 1963 he succeeded Hugh Gaitskell as Leader of the Labour Party. When Labour won the 1964 Election, he became Prime Minister, and when they lost in 1970 he led his party in opposition. In 1974 he once again became Premier and retained that post until his resignation in April 1976. He has never been out of Parliament since he first entered in 1945 and, as a consequence, he is one of the longest serving members.

Ironically, in 1908 his father was Deputy Election Agent to Winston Churchill who was then a member of the Liberal party. One of Sir Harold's proudest achievements was the foundation of Open University. It was nothing to do with the Party, it was not even in the Manifesto. In fact everybody was against it, including the Treasury who thought it wouldn't work. They didn't want to spend the money.

Sir Harold is a most courteous man and an excellent host, he is also very observant ...

During the thirty-three years in which he has sat in Parliament, he has witnessed many an aspiring young politician who has either realised both their potential and their ambition or who has subsequently fallen by the way-side. He first became aware of Margaret Thatcher when she entered the House in 1959.

'Every new lady member makes an impact on the men, especially the pretty ones,' he said with a chuckle. 'But other than that I don't think she made a great deal of

94

impact. However, she came in as a pro-Government supporter and if you are going to make your name, it's often easier to do so in Opposition. All she had to do was vote at her Party's call and never thought a thing for herself. That's no reflection on her at all, its just a quotation from Gilbert and Sullivan.' He paused for a moment to reflect on the source of these celebrated words. 'In fact it was the first Lord Sullivan, H.M. Pinafore,' he commented with an air of complete satisfaction. 'I didn't get the impression that she made many speeches during that initial period but having said that, if for example she had been speaking on education, I wouldn't normally have been in the House for that debate. I would imagine that she probably spent most of her time on committees. Within her Party as in ours there are a lot of facilities for doing work behind the scenes and she probably dedicated herself to that. She really made her impact on the House and indeed in the country when she became a member of Ted Heath's Cabinet and her great associate Sir Keith Joseph who was regarded as the hard line economist, really did a remarkable job on the health service as Secretary of State for Health.'

No one in those early days of the Heath administration could really have looked into the future and foreseen both his departure and the emergence of Margaret Thatcher as leader of the Party. 'When Heath agreed to have this system of election, which incidentally was our system and has now been adopted by everyone, I don't think for a moment that he thought he would be beaten. Indeed in the absence of somebody of substance standing against him he would undoubtedly have been elected. A lot of people who voted for Margaret did so because they didn't want Ted for various reasons and lots of others voted for her because they admired her guts. I have no doubt at all that Margaret was elected because of her courage. I agree with Lord Shinwell's view that she stood because she was the only man in the Conservative Party. Women politicians vary a great deal, as indeed do men, but you occasionally find that a woman politician is more of a man than any of the men. I would have said that of Edith Summerskill who was in the Cabinet with me in Attlee's day and I would say it's probably true of Mrs Thatcher.'

This train of thought prompted Sir Harold to meditate upon the predominant characteristics of manhood. 'To define manishness is to describe all the things that men are, like being supremely logical, cold, courageous and calculating and not soft and kittenish and all that which women are supposed to be, and aren't! Barbara Castle is the most difficult to describe because she has a great deal of charm and a great deal of ability. I remember Michael Stewart once said that she was by far the most able administrator in my Cabinet – yet though she's soft and charming with it she's ruthless when fighting the Chancellor to get what she wants. Whilst one can't really classify women, I would certainly classify Margaret Thatcher as someone who obviously possesses a great deal of feminine charm and good looks but who at the same time is as determined and relentless as any male politician.'

Whilst few politicians seem to have envisaged the possibility or even probability of having a woman as leader of one of the main parties in the nineteen seventies, Sir Harold was always convinced that this hypothesis would very soon become a reality. 'I would have put money on it and I would have put money on two persons: Barbara, who was hit partly by the fact that she wasn't in the Attlee Government, and partly by the fact that she was thirteen years in Opposition and therefore getting on a bit, and Shirley Williams who I brought into the Government very soon after she came into Parliament.'

At this juncture, the divisional bell could be heard ringing all over the House and it was time for all the MPs to scuttle into the lobby and vote. Sir Harold quickly reappeared, somewhat breathless, made his apologies very graciously and settled down again to talk about some of the procedures which are associated with the premiership.

'There has always been a practice that the Leader of the Opposition can see the Prime Minister in his room behind the Speaker's chair on the initiative of either. When I

96

Britain's first woman Prime Minister, with husband Denis after the
Conservative Party swept to power in May 1979

Right: visiting President Carter in 1979. Mrs Carter is at left; *below:* a Press conference with President Giscard D'Estaing, when the French premier visited Britain to discuss the 'Lamb War', in 1979

was Prime Minister during the sixties, Ted used to come and see me regularly about Northern Ireland and I on occasions used to go and see him on the same subject. When Margaret became leader, the discussions were once more concentrated upon the problems of Northern Ireland and when the Armagh murders occurred we reacted very strongly. I put the SAS in and then set up a consultative body of the main parties who would meet at Number 10 to review the situation. Again if I was going to set up a Royal Commission, I would naturally consult Margaret and if there were going to be MPs on it I would ask her to nominate the Conservative men or women. Whatever the occasion, I always found her approachable and easy to talk to. However, I was always aware that the wheels of her mind were turning round as she considered whether or not there was a political angle which she had better take account of before simply saying yes. Very often she would say that she was going to consult with her colleagues, which of course was a practice I used to adopt.'

In every walk of life there are those who are prepared to work hard and others who are somewhat indolent and opt for the easy life. After a lifetime in Parliament, Sir Harold has had the opportunity to observe every kind of political animal and has become something of an expert on leaders past and present, so how would he assess Margaret Thatcher's capacity to work?

'She is a very very hard worker. Of course there are lazy people in politics. You can't say Ted Heath was and I don't think anyone could say I was. Alec took it much more easily though he possessed a kind of divine right to rule together with an inherent shrewdness. Macmillan worked hard though he always pretended to be feigning but I could tell from his autobiographies and my long contact with him over the years that in fact he really did work hard. Margaret is certainly industrious and her predominant characteristic is her total dedication to the job. Although she can obviously relax, she is so dedicated that I think she eats, sleeps and dreams politics. I think she tends to be obsessive on subjects. I am not saying this in a bad way. I think politicians have a right and sometimes a duty to be obsessive about things that matter. I think she over-does the Marxist theme. On the other hand the job of a party leader who wants to win the election is to get their own party to feel strongly enough to actually turn out and vote, so to that extent she may be putting a bit of fire into them. As far as the immigration issue is concerned, I think this is something that she has done very much on her own. More than likely, I think she will probably get her own people who were in two minds about voting for her to go out and vote, she may be strengthening the vote of her own people who are probably prejudiced in that way anyway, rather than making new converts. But she is taking some risks in losing the vote of the immigrant population. When it comes to city manners, and as you know I'm very in-volved in the city myself at the moment, she certainly knows what she is talking about. She did in fact have a stint on the economic side and I think that her knowledge particularly in the field of taxation and its various ramifi-cations and refinements is very good indeed. In my opinion, she would have made a very good Chancellor of the Exchequer. In addition, she is extremely good on the Finance Bill, committee stage, when you are talking about the finesse of taxation changes. As far as general economics are concerned, I think for her it's more theoretical but she certainly knows a good deal about the kind of economic philosophy she likes. I should imagine she knows her Friedman very well but needless to say my views on the subject do not coincide with hers.'

'Philosophies and doctrines apart, how important or indeed relevant is a person's basic education and back-ground in the political arena?'

'Margaret's training quite apart from her youthful experiences which are also very important are a definite advantage to a politician, particularly a Conservative politician. I am thinking especially of her legal training which has probably sharpened both her mind and her argumentative capacity in the realms of debate. She appears a little like a barrister on many occasions in that

98

she can see the weakness of the other case and the strength of her own. In her present capacity, this is undoubtedly a help and I believe her scientific training gives her an added advantage.'

Just as brevity is the sole of wit, the shorter the speech, the more poignant may be the message. The art of speech making is a difficult one which few people have managed to master and the pressures of Parliament provide a formidable test.

'Margaret doesn't often get laughs with her speeches but she can be a very effective speaker on a motion of censure. She has also learnt to do something which few politicians manage to achieve and I certainly never learnt to do, namely to produce on a set piece occasion a very short and effective speech just to get the main points across. She accomplishes this quite easily in half an hour as opposed to the customary forty-five or fifty minutes.'

Praise indeed from one of the all time great speech makers, who paused for a moment to reflect upon some of her other characteristics.

'I think she is feminine and dignified and I don't think she consciously says that because I am a woman I have to appear more mannish – I think the sharpness of her brain makes her what she is. Although the Tory Party do less on hunch and feel than ours and rely more on their surveys, their advice and their public relations firms, I do think that Margaret has a hunch and feel, and she is naturally at her happiest when her hunch proves to be right. I would certainly think that she would be a good listener. When she meets people on walkabouts, she always appears to be interested in what they have to say. She may or may not be bored but she definitely doesn't show it. She knows that a politician has to take infinite trouble with people and I think in a sense she does take infinite trouble with their views. It's a different party to ours and more would be happening in her room than would be happening in the Labour leader's room. She would also have to attend a lot more dinner parties than I did and I can remember when I became leader and John Strachey asked me out straight

99

away and I said, "No John, you can afford to give dinners, but my job is here and my room is going to be open so that any MP can come in and I shall be here every evening and dine in the Commons dining room." '

For some unaccountable reason, the conversation progressed from the delicacies of the House to a discourse on the similarities or otherwise between the leadership of Margaret Thatcher and Ted Heath.

'Their leadership is very different although I could think of Conservative leaders who were more different from both of them than they are from each other. Macmillan is an example. Ted was utterly dedicated and had no other interests except for his music and sailing which he took up rather late in life. Not having a wife and children to go home to, he has never been preoccupied with the everyday problems of family life such as the traumas involved when the children get chicken pox and measles when you have to forget all the in-fighting and arguments and this is an advantage to a politician. Margaret on the other hand has obviously had to cope with all the responsibilities of being a wife and mother. However she and Ted do have one important characteristic in common – their dedication to the job and there are other ways too in which they are alike. Margaret is more tolerant and I think she will certainly listen to people even if her mind is made up. Ted would give the impression that there was only one doctrine on the subject and that was his and he would regard it as a waste of time to discuss it. I always get the impression that the Conservative Party elect their leader and then take him over. They package him, they shape his hair and then whisk him off to the tailors if the colour doesn't suit him. I am quite sure this is literally true, but Margaret has allowed them to shape her much less than Ted did. In the first place, you *can't* quite imagine the Tory chieftains telling her how to do her hair or how to dress – they just wouldn't know! A lady knows much more about these things, she knows what styles and colours suit her. Accordingly, even on that narrow sphere, I don't think the Tories know what to do

100

with her and it's as well for her that they don't. On speech matters too I think she would insist rather more than Ted, and I would be surprised if she let them rehearse her too much. Talking of rehearsals and broadcasting, I was the first politician ever to use auto-cue. Against all the advice of the BBC I insisted upon it. Ted followed in my footsteps and although I've no proof of this I'm sure his party rehearsed him over and over again.'

Sir Harold has had the unique opportunity of observing Margaret Thatcher both in his capacity as Prime Minister and latterly in his more unusual role as a back bencher. Was she the best choice as leader and how would he assess her standing in the party after three years in office?

'Yes I think she was the best choice in the circumstances. I can't think of anyone better. She is certainly well established. Anyone suggesting that she should be replaced would fail to get any support except perhaps from half a dozen disgruntled people who haven't been brought on to the front bench lately. Of course any one of those who tried to replace her would get the full Tory treatment which is much more brutal than anything that happens in the Labour Party — boiling oil, the lot! This however is not what is keeping her there. She is a very very astute politician who has established herself with the Party and has been totally accepted by them as their leader.

Margaret is much more ideological than any Conservative leader I've ever known. It's both an intellectual and moral ideology. Her belief in free markets and free enterprise is social as well as intellectual. She had a strict moral upbringing whose existence depended upon hard work and private enterprise. I would think therefore that what she is convinced of intellectually, she also believes in morally as the right thing to do. She thinks communism is an evil. She is always talking about the communist members in this country but as I said at the weekend, we haven't any now except for a few ageing types in the coalfields. The problem is the Trotskyites who for example made their presence felt at Grunwick, and I have made speeches about them for years both as Prime Minister and since I resigned that

101

office in 1976.'

'Where do the Trotskyites make their presence felt – have they infiltrated the Labour Party?'

'Yes. The Newham constituency is a case in point. They move into bed sitters, into an area where there is a Labour seat but a relatively small party and then they take over the party by getting their friends elected. They have a big hold among the young people and they can be found on the fringe of journalism, the fringe of broadcasting and certain magazines. The difference between the Trotskyite and the communist is that the communist wants to set up a society based on Stalin or Lenin. The Trotskyites are passionately opposed to that – all they want to do is to destroy the system of society. They run under different aliases, which they change from time to time. Margaret tends to lump them all together.'

'Harold Macmillan said of Margaret Thatcher, 'She will make a very good Prime Minister, I'm certain.' If she became Prime Minister, would the fact that she is a woman make any difference?'

'Not at all. In many ways people would be quite pleased, certainly a little intrigued and there would be an air of some excitement. The fact that she is a woman would be a novelty which would wear off very quickly and in no time at all she would be judged by what she was doing, what her policies were, how she carried them out and who she appointed. She would stand or fall solely on that. She would be no more likely to get pushed out in a hurry because she is a woman and no more likely to be kept if they thought she was a failure. As I said in my two most recent books, the Tory party is ruthless with its leaders. They never actually talk about getting rid of their leader, then suddenly there is a flash of steel between the shoulder blades and rigor mortis sets in.'

The interview drew to a close, Sir Harold hospitably offered me a glass of sherry and much to Mike Yarwood's regret didn't once mention what he had said at the Brighton conference.

A. Neave – 'She's the first real idealist politician for a long time.'

The late Airey Neave was the MP for Abingdon and the Opposition Front Bench Spokesman on Northern Ireland. He was born in London of an English father and an Irish mother. He studied to become a barrister before war broke out in 1939 and was taken prisoner by the Germans at Calais in 1940. He escaped from Colditz and returned to England in May 1942. He was called to the Bar whilst still in uniform in 1943 and subsequently went back to France having organised the underground escape lines for the RAF. In 1945, he went to Nuremberg as a judicial aid to the Nuremberg Tribunal and served the indictment on the top Nazis such as Hess and Speer, in their cells. He was the assistant secretary of the Tribunal for a year and in 1946 he returned to England and started to practice at the Bar. He remained in practice for nine years and during that time he stood for Parliament twice. It was in those circumstances that in 1950 he first met Margaret Thatcher, then Margaret Roberts, who was the Parliamentary candidate for Dartford.

When I met Airey Neave before his tragic death in 1979 he told me how well he had come to know and respect Margaret Thatcher over the previous twenty-eight years.

He explained that during the 1950 Parliament, candidates tended to meet frequently and Margaret Thatcher was one of the people he came to know best. He found her very friendly and easy to talk to and soon began to realise that she was extremely intelligent and hard working – later he was to discover that she was more than that.

In 1953, Margaret Thatcher passed the Bar finals and qualified as a barrister. She then spent a year doing a common law pupillage in Lord Justice Lawton's chambers where Airey Neave was a junior tenant. He recalls that during that period she spent most of her time doing criminal cases before transferring to tax chambers. 'She subsequently became very expert in tax and is now one of the best informed people on taxation questions in this country.' Although at that time it was undoubtedly very unusual for a woman to be a tenant in tax chambers, as indeed it was at the common law bar, he felt there wasn't much prejudice against women among the barristers themselves. Airey Neave feels that there is a similar lack of prejudice against women in the House of Commons. 'This is not a place where women aren't treated equally as colleagues. They are and have been for many years since Lady Astor.' However, if women don't encounter any real prejudice within the confines of the House, the attitude towards lady politicians outside those walls is somewhat different. As Airey Neave remembers, Margaret Thatcher had quite a struggle to get a seat and on more than one occasion was told by the Select Committee to go home and mind her children. When she was finally adopted for Finchley, it was entirely on her own merits. Speaking of the difficulties which women politicians face in various parts of the country, Airey Neave focused his attention on the struggle for the Conservative Party leadership in 1975.

As Margaret Thatcher's campaign manager he spoke of the surprise that some people experienced over the MPs' choice of a *woman* as leader of their party – after all, it was an innovation in British politics. He went on to say that over the past three years these areas of scepticism have started to diminish and now it's beginning to be accepted that she really has been chosen on her merits – as the most gifted politician we have in the Conservative Party and perhaps *the* most gifted politician for twenty-five years. 'She's the first real idealist politician for a long time. Macmillan might have been the last in the Conservative Party – there may have been others on the other side of the House but Margaret is a philosopher as well as a politician.'

Mr Neave then philosophised in his own way about Margaret Thatcher as a person. He described her as an approachable, rather understanding person who despite the enormous pressures of work managed to find time to talk to everyone. Apparently, one of her first acts on becoming leader was to tell the Party that she would always be ready to talk and she has carried out that pledge faithfully ever since. He feels strongly that the descriptions which have been attributed to her at various times in the past – descriptions of her as being cold, extreme, toffee-nosed and suburban bear not the slightest resemblance to the real Margaret Thatcher. 'They are all complete nonsense,' he said. 'Far from being cold or extreme about anything,' she is a compassionate, patient and very well balanced person who has an affinity with people and a clear understanding of the opinions of men and women in the street.' He believes that she has a personal magnetism of a kind that few political leaders in Britain have had and although she had been criticised for her statement and subsequent stand on immigration, he thinks that she has struck exactly the right note because she knows what people feel and echoed the majority view.

'Although she is serious by nature and as a great patriot is very concerned about the future of this country, there is a humorous side to her and off duty she can be very amusing and has the ability to laugh at herself. She is self-critical, likes accuracy, enjoys a well reasoned argument and respects people who know their facts – she has immense powers of concentration and a quite exceptional memory. When it comes to labour Prime Ministers who don't know the answers,' relates Airey Neave, 'they come in for a very rough time indeed. I've known no Leader of the Opposition during the twenty-five years in which I've been in Parliament who is as strong as she is in dealing with the Prime Minister of the day. Her court experience has undoubtedly helped to make her a formidable cross-examiner and she always has her case well prepared.'

Finally, I asked Airey Neave whether he could single out any one predominant characteristic in Margaret

Thatcher. 'I would choose her great personal courage. It may be that she has many frightening experiences to come but the thing she will never lack is courage. That is her great quality. She is outspoken by nature and is essentially a fighter and nobody should be surprised if she tells the country a few home truths.'

Jill Knight – 'Sometimes she's very hurt, her armour is not such as to be impenetrable.'

Jill Knight is the Conservative MP for Edgbaston. She was born in Bristol and is married with two children. She first became interested in politics at the age of thirteen when her schoolteacher, a keen and earnest Fabian who saw it as her duty in life to teach all of her charges to be keen and earnest Fabians, introduced the class to a book by William Morris. She was so appalled by its description of the golden age of socialism (where money was an out-moded class symbol and everyone worked for the State, where neither the house you lived in nor the clothes you stood up in were actually yours, and where the children belonged to the State and were looked after by the State) that she decided from that moment on she had to be on the other side.

She first entered the House of Commons twelve years ago and said of herself, 'I'm not a bra-burning women's libber because I think that any woman who is really determined enough can make it. I don't want a woman to get somewhere because she is a woman. What interests me is that she should get somewhere because she is capable and I'm afraid that means *in spite* of being a woman.'

Jill Knight has an outgoing personality and as one of the few women in the party, has come to know Margaret Thatcher very well over the past sixteen years. She disclosed that she hadn't anticipated a woman becoming leader of the Conservative Party in her political lifetime and felt that this view was shared by the average man and woman in the street who hadn't foreseen such a possibility. 'Again if you had asked me even five years ago, whether there would be a female Prime Minister and if so, who would she be, I'm ashamed to say, I would have replied that I don't think there will be a female PM but should it happen, it will probably be Shirley Williams. She seemed at that point to be much nearer the premiership than Margaret.'

However, following the defeat of the Conservative Party in the 1974 election, and the ensuing question mark over the leadership, she felt that if Margaret Thatcher had been a man there would have been no question at all about her being chosen as leader – none! The problem was to get over the reactionary feeling towards women. Some of the men in the party had an instinctive gut reaction to the prospect of having a woman as their leader and there was resentment against Margaret solely because she was a woman.

'I believe that this resentment has been overcome and that ninety-eight per cent of the Party, namely colleagues in the House, are absolutely rock solid behind her.'

'Is there any resentment towards her among other women in the House?'

'I can honestly say I have never noticed any at all. The women here are not particularly close. We don't do anything as women members. I think this is right. We have just as wide differences between us politically as we have with any of the men. Frankly, some of the women in this place are out and out Marxists and no way am I going to mix with them!'

Speaking of women in politics generally, she explained that whilst women undoubtedly have many disadvantages to overcome, in one particular sphere the female politician does have a distinct advantage. Namely, she is constantly brought down from her perch by the small domestic details which the men simply don't have to cope with. 'When I go back home on weekends, I have to cook the meals, do the

107

shopping and make sure the washing is done. Now I would lay you any money you like that it scarcely ever enters a man's head as to whether or not there are sufficient chops in the fridge or enough clean underwear for the week. The small domestic details that women have to busy themselves with might be thought to be trivia by men but that so-called trivia plays an important part in making and keeping you human. Frankly, too many politicians get too big for their boots. They get to the point where they are rather above the thought of getting on a bus or even going to a supermarket. Politicians are there to represent the people in their constituency. If an MP doesn't know what it's like to have to cope with looking after the children, fetching them from school and doing the shopping in that particular area then a gulf develops between the MP and the constituents. Consequently, although women politicians do have several obstacles to surmount, they also have a few plusses, and I certainly think this is one of them. Margaret is more in touch with the ordinary everyday person. She is still very domesticated. She still cooks the breakfast for the family. She still tidies up and puffs up all the cushions. The domestic side plays and always has played a very important part in her life.'

Most people resent their strongly held views being opposed, but how does Margaret Thatcher react in those circumstances?

'I've never known her round angrily on anyone, that doesn't mean to say she's never done it, it's just that she's never done it while I've been around. She will always listen and see whether there's any merit in what you say. I've never known her to be really impatient with anyone, but again that doesn't mean to say that she never has.'

In the past, backbenchers have sometimes complained of the difficulty of getting the ear of their leader. Does this still apply?

'One of Margaret's great and very special attributes as a leader is that she listens so carefully to what you say. She gives you her whole attention. If you have a problem or an idea you want to put forward, she will always listen because she is genuinely interested in it. She is very, very approachable and I think all members feel like this about Margaret. I believe that a great political figure has to be two things: awe-inspiring on the one side and yet immensely human and approachable on the other. To be really great they have to inspire not only respect but affection.'

'What other facets of her character are you especially aware of?'

'Her fantastic brain and her overall grasp of multifarious problems. For example when she was Secretary of State for Education, I took a deputation from Birmingham to see her. They were stunned not only by the way she grasped so rapidly the essentials of the arguments which they were putting to her but equally by the extremely probing questions she put to them. At that time in some local authorities, we had the question of comprehensivisation in schools being pushed forward. Now my constituency is in Birmingham, but frankly I don't know how many schools there are in that area, there must be hundreds, but Margaret knew. When the delegates mentioned a particular school, much to their amazement, she knew exactly what the problems were there. For instance she knew exactly what would happen if two particular schools were amalgamated. She even knew the exact distance between them. When she had to look at these schemes, she really did look at them. An awful lot of ministers leave it to their permanent staff, not Margaret. She also has a quiet dignity which I happen to believe is still important in a leader. I think a great many people in Britain would like to get back to the point where we have leaders who look like leaders, who talk like leaders, who think like leaders, who behave like leaders and who judge like leaders. Allied to this she has a tremendous blazing honesty and a compassionate concern for people generally.'

Most politicians are subjected to both personal and political attacks, such is the nature of the role. Margaret Thatcher, perhaps partly due to her unique position in British politics, has attracted her fair share of criticism.

109

But how does it affect her? How often is the armour pierced?

'You don't get into Parliament without realising that you are going to be criticised by people who for no personal reason detest you. Some people have political axes to grind and will do everything they can to make you unhappy and I think Margaret has had more than her fair share of this. There are the purely feminine observations too and it irritates me beyond bearing that no one ever says, "I don't like the way Jim Callaghan does his hair." Margaret like every other politician knows that she is going to be criticised but that doesn't mean that the criticism doesn't occasionally upset and hurt her, I'm sure it does. Sometimes, she's very hurt, her armour is not such as to be impenetrable by these shafts.'

Fergus Montgomery – 'Her ultimate decision to stand wasn't prompted by any desire to hurt Heath.'

Fergus Montgomery, a former schoolmaster, has been the Conservative MP for Altrincham and Sale since 1974. This prematurely white-haired Geordie, who has never lost a trace of his dialect, has been in Parliament since 1959. When he entered the House, it was in a blaze of glory. 'That's my one claim to fame, I was the only Tory ever to win Newcastle-on-Tyne East. I won by ninety-eight votes which was too close for comfort and in 1964 I lost the seat.' In 1967, he won the by-election at Brierley Hill, a seat which he held until 1974. It was then that the Boundary Commissioners redistributed that constituency thereby taking in more Labour voters than a Tory could be expected to cope with and in February 1974 he lost the seat. Six months later he returned to Parliament as MP for the constituency he now holds.

He first met Margaret Thatcher in 1959 when they both made their debut in the House of Commons. He recalled that she and a man called Monty Woodhouse, the MP for Oxford, were the first two of the 1959 intake to be given jobs by Harold Macmillan. She was made the Joint Parliamentary Secretary to the Ministry of Pensions and National Insurance. It was apparent to him early on in the 1959/64 Parliament that she had enormous ability and was likely to go a long way. However, he never imagined either in 1959 or even in later years that the day would ever dawn when she would become leader of the Party. It was almost inconceivable that the 'staid old Conservative Party would have been the first party in this country to have a woman as their leader.'

It wasn't until 1969 when Margaret Thatcher became Shadow Spokesman for Education and Fergus Montgomery was appointed to the Committee that he came to know her really well and experienced at first hand her infinite capacity to work. 'She led the attack on the Education Bill that Edward Short was trying to put through to force a totally comprehensive system. We managed to defeat them on an all-important clause and they had to start from scratch, but in the meantime the 1970 election took place and the whole thing fell to the ground.'

In 1970, Ted Heath appointed Margaret Thatcher as Secretary of State for Education and in 1973, Fergus Montgomery was appointed as her PPS – 'or as some would say,' he laughed, 'pretty poor substitute !' Being the PPS to the only lady in the Cabinet had its problems. Other PPSs used to refer rather jocularly to their masters but he could scarcely refer to her as his mistress for fear of being misunderstood. 'It was during that period that I became aware of her analytical mind, her ability to get to the root of a problem and to make a decision and the pure down-to-earth logic of her reasoning. But above all I was touched by her compassion, and her real concern for

111

people.' In later years, he was to personally experience just how genuine that concern was.

When Labour won the election in October 1974 and a question mark over the future leadership of the Conservative Party arose, Fergus Montgomery was one of the people who tried to persuade Margaret Thatcher to stand. 'Her initial response to the suggestion was "no" for she felt that the Party wasn't ready to have a female leader. Her ultimate decision to stand wasn't prompted by any desire to hurt Heath – far from it! She stood because somebody had to stand and all the men fell by the wayside. She was the lady who had the guts to do it. If she had lost it could have been the kiss of death for her, politically.'

But even during this tense situation, there was time for a little humour. On the second ballot for the leadership contest, there was a picture in all the papers of Willie Whitelaw kissing Margaret on the promenade. Mr Whitelaw's response to the publication of these pictures drew a burst of laughter from Mrs T. Apparently he had said, 'I don't know what they're making all this fuss about, after all, we've done it so many times before. We've done it in the street, we've done it in hotels . . . '

For the first year that Margaret Thatcher was leader of the Opposition, Fergus Montgomery was again appointed as her PPS. The work was very tiring and time-consuming but it was also rewarding because he was at the centre of things. 'Nothing ever happened during that period that didn't enhance my respect for her and I think that anybody who has ever worked in her private office since she became leader would vouch for the same thing. She's thoughtful, she's kind and you get this aura of working in the presence of someone with exceptional ability. Her great belief is that you really only learn by listening to other people's views. If you close your mind to their views, then you close your mind to knowledge.

'A lot of people, and I think this is a very valid point, who start off as rather nice people suddenly do very well and it all goes to their head. They haven't got their feet on the ground any more and tend to become rather big

112

headed. This has not happened in the case of Margaret Thatcher. With her there are no airs. She is exactly the same as she was all those years ago !'

Finally, Fergus Montgomery talked about one of the most harrowing experiences of his life. On one bleak Monday in 1977, he was charged with taking two books from a London store. Before 8 o'clock on the Tuesday morning, he received a phone call from Margaret Thatcher, a person who was to remain his friend throughout this traumatic episode. She was anxious to discover what his plans were for the day and he told her that he had to go to court but that afterwards he would be going straight home since he couldn't face the prospect of seeing other people. She eventually persuaded him to go to the House of Commons for she felt that he had to face that hurdle at some time and the longer he put it off the worse it would become. She subsequently re-arranged her engagements for the day, apart from PM's question time and asked Fergus to go and see her. After a long talk, she suddenly said, 'Come on, we're going for a walk.' She then walked him round all the corridors of the building so that people could see that he was with her. Having exhausted all the corridors, she ushered him into the members' tea room where she sat with him for an hour so that anyone coming in could see them sitting together. When the case was eventually heard in September, things went wrong and Margaret Thatcher was the first person on the telephone. The following December, the case went to Appeal and Fergus Montgomery was totally acquitted of the charge. He left the court with his wife, Joyce, returned to the House of Commons and went into the bar. He was on the point of telephoning Mrs Thatcher to tell her the news when his wife said, 'Don't bother, here she is.'

'In all the years I've known her, I've never seen her in the bar. She simply walked past everybody, came over, flung her arms round me, gave me a kiss and said "I don't have to tell you, do I." '

Andrew Faulds – 'That bloody woman!'

Andrew Faulds was born in Africa and described himself as 'coming from a very responsible professional Scottish background.' He is the Labour Member of Parliament for Warley East. He is a former actor, whose performances have ranged from Stratford on Avon to radio's *Journey into Space*. Prior to entering the House, Mr Faulds had appeared in over thirty films and has also acted in a number of TV dramas. 'I gave up acting full time in 1966 when I became an MP. I've done a bit since but only within the limitations of what my duty as a politician allows. That is my first commitment.' Andrew Faulds is a volatile critic of Margaret Thatcher. It was he who referred to her as 'that bloody woman' during Parliamentary proceedings. Of course there have been political feuds and vendettas throughout the history of our democracy. Stories of battles in the House followed by drinks in the bar are legendary. There is, however, nothing cosy about the Faulds/Thatcher confrontations of which there have been several. He explained the 'bloody woman' episode.

'I thought her handling of the immigration issue in that Granada TV interview was totally irresponsible, totally unprincipled and very damaging for areas like mine at Smethwick, where many of us have worked hard to make good community relations. Her use of the issue and the use of emotional phrases like being "swamped" was quite disgraceful.'

Did he feel that immigration was a big issue in society today?

'I don't think so. By and large in Smethwick we have good community relations. I am perhaps lucky in that I have a Sikh community, who are, like the Scots, extremely hard-working and have a very low crime rate, much lower than the native population. Whether we like it or not Britain is now a multi racial society. Some people see their High Streets changing. They see a lot of Indian shops set up but they're being set up of course in decaying areas. That's what complicates the problems. Indians move in because they can't get shops in better areas. The answer to that is not to adopt racialist slogans but to try and integrate the coloured section of our community into other areas. I would be very happy if a lot of those people who were parked four deep in some of the streets in my constituency were to move out to sunnier climes like Cheltenham and Stratford on Avon.'

Mr Faulds felt that in making her stand on immigration Margaret Thatcher hadn't considered the damage this would do to her own prospects in areas where the immigrant community now decide who wins the election. He was obviously genuinely concerned for his constituency and for the large coloured section contained therein. 'I had the great joy, because of my African background, of winning it back from the Conservatives on an anti-racialist ticket – I'm violently anti-racialist!'

We returned to the subject of Margaret Thatcher.

'I think she may need to put up a tough appearance to compensate for the fact that she's not a man, but in doing that she seems to have lost a lot of female compassion. I don't see her as having much sensitivity towards other people. Politics is more naturally a man's world. I think some women hold their own very well but I think they lessen their femininity and womanhood by holding their own very well – she's one of them. To be fair to her, she has a great deal of regard for the law and I think she would certainly want to see equality before the law for all members of the British community whatever their colour. However, I find myself very much out of sympathy with her.'

Had Mr Faulds ever met her socially?

'No, I don't have the pleasure of knowing her at all on a

115

personal basis ! We've never even had a drink or a cup of tea ! I know her only as a political animal across the floor of the House.'

William Whitelaw – 'I found her ... well rather frightening.'

The Rt Hon William Whitelaw, MC, has been the Conservative MP for Penrith since 1955. He has been Deputy Leader of the Opposition and Spokesman on Home Affairs and Devolution since 1975. He served under the Heath administration in various capacities including that of Lord President of the Council, Leader of the House and Secretary of State for Northern Ireland. Willie Whitelaw is a popular figure with most members of the House of Commons, his amiable personality is quite disarming. Although he first met Margaret Thatcher in 1959 when she entered the House, he scarcely knew her until they were both junior ministers in the Government of 1962–1964. But even then he didn't know her particularly well, so what were his early impressions?

'I found her enormously able, very competent and at that time before I really got to know her well rather frightening.'

'Frightening?'

'Yes. Well at that stage, I was one of those people who was always rather frightened of women politicians. I don't know why, I just was. I was rather frightened by her immense competence and knowledge. Back in those days, that would have been the view of many members towards female MPs. It's very different now of course.'

After this somewhat intimidating impact, when if at all, did they become better acquainted?

116

'I didn't know her very well in Cabinet and I didn't really know her personally until she became Leader. Of course, over the past three years, I've got to know her extremely well and we've become great friends. I admire her enormously. You couldn't as a woman have become Leader of the Party unless you had enormous determination and enormous dedication. You couldn't conceivably have worked as a chemist, had twins, qualified as a barrister, stood as a candidate and got into Parliament without these two qualities.'

'Are there any inherent problems having a woman as Leader? Is there perhaps even a subconscious reaction to a woman at the helm?'

'No, not at all — not at all! I think that everybody accepts it as a perfectly normal state of affairs. I don't find it odd in any way and I don't think it presents any problems whatsoever. I have no hesitation in telling her what I think and thanks to her, we have an excellent relationship.'

'Thanks to her?'

'I say that because she had to make the initial approach. At the time I was merely an acquaintance. She had to deal with someone who had stood against her for the Leadership. In addition it was alleged, somewhat wrongly in certain cases, that I had a different outlook on many things to her. But she made her mind up – she was going to get on with me. I made my mind up – I was going to get on with her. That's why I say thanks to her because she did everything she could to make it easy for me.'

Over the past three years, has he found more common ground in terms of outlook and beliefs? Do many of his ideas and philosophies coincide with hers?

'A great many more than I ever expected. We are different in as much as we're in a slightly different age group. I was in the army throughout the war which has a considerable effect on your outlook. I was almost grown up in the thirties. We have different backgrounds and I've led a very different life to her. I'm a Northerner and very interested in country sports, she's not. She's a voracious reader, I'm not. We don't have many of the same interests but we do get on frightfully well together.'

'Is she easy to communicate with? Is she receptive to your views – a good listener?'

'On a personal level yes, she's very easy to talk to. She's less easy with a group. In a group, she's very clear what she wants to get out of them and is inclined to talk quite a lot. But she will listen very profoundly individually, or with a few people.'

'How does she react when you express an opposing view?'

'Alone, very well. In a group, where she's determined to get her way, she's inclined not to listen but to keep on hammering her point home, but she does listen in the end. She's a little intolerant of views which have already been rejected – I don't blame her for that, so am I. She finds it difficult to listen to the same views over and over again. In the Shadow Cabinet, for example, if she doesn't like the view that somebody's putting forward, she can shoot it down pretty quickly. She can shoot people down and she can be very tough in argument but after all, any Leader has got to do that otherwise they wouldn't be Leaders. Every Leader has to have a certain amount of steel otherwise they would be pushed around. However, I would have thought that the members of the Shadow Cabinet find it easy to work for her because she is a very good listener individually.'

'Is she easy going?'

'Not easy going, no. Because she sets very high standards and they have to be met. She has great determination and great drive and therefore naturally she's not easy going.'

'Does she possess the ability to grasp the essentials of a problem with alacrity?'

'Oh yes, absolutely. She has an enormously quick mind and a very flexible one. There is nothing rigid about her at all. If you argue a case with her and she sees it makes sense and has merit, you can change her mind. She's not in the least bit rigid and committed to one line at all costs. She is very adaptable.'

'It's been said that Margaret Thatcher listens to people's personal problems and difficulties more than other leaders. Is that a justified observation?'

'Yes, I think that's certainly true – absolutely. She spends ages and ages listening to individual Members of Parliament all day long. She exhausts herself at times by having these individual interviews and listening to their various points of view. She's extremely sympathetic and very kind. If people have personal problems, she will make time to listen to them and try and make sure that they're not hustled in the political sphere. It's often said that women in politics are very hard – the very last thing you could ever say about Margaret Thatcher is that she's hard. I sometimes think she's too kind and too sympathetic. She does things in a different way to Ted Heath. Ted is a very reserved, rather distant man, not to people like me who know him very well, you break through. Margaret's much easier. The backbenchers find it much easier to talk to Margaret than they did to Ted. She is prepared to listen and is much less reserved than he was. Ted had great charm to those who knew him well. She has natural charm with people whether they know her or not. You had to break through with Ted, you don't with Margaret.'

'How would you describe Jim Callaghan's approach to Margaret Thatcher in the House?'

'I think he tries to play the part of the man in charge : "I know it all, you really haven't got the experience that I have." He tries to play the big man, the avuncular man, the quiet man, the sort of man you can trust and there's this woman coming along trying to tell you things but don't bother about her, trust me. That's his line but I think he would attempt the same approach with a man.'

'How different, if at all, is the man to the image as portrayed on the media?'

'He is totally different. He's very petulant if things go wrong, very touchy and very quick tempered, as anyone who deals with him in a TV studio or that sort of thing will know. If you want to know about the real James Callaghan, read the Crossman Diaries.'

'But what about Margaret Thatcher? Apart from those traits which have already been referred to, what facet of her nature is particularly striking?'

'One of her most remarkable characteristics is the amount of work she puts in. The little sleep she has. The fact that she manages to run a home, work at the Commons from early morning to late at night, and spend hours and hours writing speeches. She works fantastically hard. How she manages to fit all this into her day, I can't imagine. Her stamina is quite amazing. Any idea that a woman hasn't got as much stamina as a man is quite wrong. She's got twice as much stamina. She could quite easily kill me in a day with the amount she's able to do! When she goes on these walkabouts, she exhausts everybody round her and is still absolutely fresh at the end of the day.'

'Women are supposed to be gifted with intuition. Does Margaret Thatcher possess that feminine instinct?'

'Her instincts are extraordinary. I've known her to go to a by-election and come away saying quite the opposite to what all the pundits were predicting. For instance, she came back from the by-election at Ashfield, where we needed a really enormous swing, saying she thought we were going to win it. "Don't be so silly," I said. No one thought we would win but we did and she was right – she frequently is.'

'Is she firmly established as the Leader?'

'Yes, totally – absolutely no doubt about it. Of course the Leader of the Opposition is a very difficult task because it's a critical role rather than a creative one.'

'Should she become Prime Minister, what difference would it make to the people of this country, if any?'

'I think she would give us a fresh start. She has a truly remarkable knowledge of the British people. She knows what they want and has the determination to carry it through!'

Once again the division bell rang. Willie Whitelaw rose courteously and beamed, 'I'm afraid I've got to go and vote again – terribly sorry.'

Lord Thorneycroft – 'She doesn't harp back on past errors. She goes forward all the time.'

George Edward Peter Thorneycroft is the son of the late Major George Thorneycroft and Dorothy Hope, who was the daughter of Sir William Franklyn. He is married to Countess Carla Roberti and was educated at Eton and the Royal Military Academy at Woolwich. He was commissioned in the Royal Artillery in 1930 and subsequently resigned his commission in 1933. In 1935 he was called to the Bar and practised for several years on the Oxford circuit. He first entered the House of Commons in 1938 as MP for Stafford.

It was a dark, bleak, wet afternoon when I made my way towards Smith Square, which houses the headquarters of the two major parties. The grey stone buildings, elegant reminders of a bygone age, are very similar in appearance and I climbed the steps, entered the foyer of what I assumed to be Conservative Central Office and announced I had an appointment with Lord Thorneycroft.

'He doesn't often come here,' said a harassed-looking gentlemen. 'This is Transport House.' With a bemused expression on his face, he pointed me in the opposite direction, namely to No 32.

When I entered the room situated on the first floor of a large rambling building, Lord Thorneycroft, referred to simply as 'The Chairman' by all the residents of Central Office, was seated at the end of a long highly polished table. Like all efficient chairmen he was immersed in a sea of papers and a ridiculous thought crossed my mind as to whether or not he would slide a jar of marmalade down

121

the table as per the TV commercial. But this Pythonesque reverie was suddenly broken. 'Sit down,' beamed the Chairman and I did as I was bid. He seemed somewhat surprised at my interest in his political career.

'My political career? Well, it's too long and I don't think you really want to go over the whole of it. In fact I would find the very greatest difficulty in doing so because my memory for dates isn't too good. It was suggested to me – I think by a Socialist solicitor – that I should stand for Stafford and I agreed. I was a member of that constituency for a number of years up until the end of the war and then I lost Stafford in the Labour landslide of 1945, but was re-elected almost immediately afterwards as MP for Monmouth.

'I was first given office by Winston Churchill as Under-Secretary for Transport and when the Conservatives were returned to power in 1951, Winston, who was Prime Minister, brought me into the Cabinet as President of the Board of Trade. I was then the youngest member of his Cabinet. I held office for approximately six years and on reflection it was probably the position which gave me most enjoyment. On Winston's retirement I became Chancellor of the Exchequer under the premiership of Harold MacMillan and the history of that episode is well known. I eventually resigned from that office along with Enoch Powell and Nigel Birch – now Lord Rhyl – on the broad theme that the Government was spending too much money. I was then out of office, though not out of politics, for some years and was brought back by Harold MacMillan as Minister for Aviation and subsequently as Secretary of State for Defence.

'During that period the Conservatives were voted out of office and I lost my Monmouth constituency – in fact I never returned to Parliament again and was subsequently made a Life Peer. I then worked in industry, but was brought back into politics by Margaret Thatcher as Chairman of the Conservative Party. In February 1980, I completed five years in that office, which I believe is the longest time anybody has been Chairman since Lord Woolton.'

122

What persuaded Lord Thorneycroft to return to the frenetic hustings of political life after an absence of more than ten years? Was the change of leadership an important and contributory factor?

'Well, obviously I wouldn't have returned to politics if Margaret hadn't asked me. In addition, I had no doubt that she was the right Leader of the Conservative Party. They needed the drive and faith which even then she so obviously possessed. Of course, the qualities for which she is respected today were not so apparent then. She was untried, she was virtually unknown. She had only held two major offices – pensions and education – so she obviously hadn't had a chance to prove herself at that time, but to any of those who knew her she possessed undoubted qualities. There weren't very many people in the Conservative Party who were obvious leadership material and I think the whole Party is delighted with the way their choice has turned out.'

'Leadership is that ingredient of personality which causes men to follow,' said H. S. Gilbertson. Lord Thorneycroft has held key positions in three very different administrations. Was it possible to draw any direct comparison between the varying personalities and style of these distinctive leaders?

'They all differ so very widely from one another that it's almost impossible to make comparisons. People don't become Prime Minister without very great merits: you don't just stumble into the job. Winston would never have been Prime Minister had it not been for the war. He held views and violent political opinions which were offensive to large sections of the Conservative Party. When I first went into the House of Commons I used to be warned by the whips about the dangers of following Winston Churchill and this was only a few years before he became a national hero. Winston wasn't popular with the Establishment. He had been a Liberal and had adhered to Liberal practices. But he was a man who found his great strength in the sheer size of the adversities which threatened this country.

123

'Harold MacMillan was probably the most intellectual, educated, cultured and thoughtful Prime Minister that I've served under – he saw everything against a great backlog of history. He was a very distinguished man, as indeed he is today. He is still probably one of the most delightful commentators and conversationalists on political matters around, but they all possess great gifts. Margaret Thatcher has great courage and tremendous determination, which are characteristics she shares in common with Winston – If she sees something which needs to be done, she goes all out for it, though it's important to mention that she is, in fact, more cautious than she's given credit for.

'Women tend to be more cautious than men, they have a tendency to think rather more carefully before embarking upon a particular course of action and this is a trait Margaret has in common with other women. She is quite careful about the way she comes to a decision and she's a very hard worker at her decisions. Nevertheless, once she has made a decision she goes for the solution with immense vigour. She is brilliantly briefed, she's read the brief and she knows all the facts, so you inevitably get into certain difficulties if you are not fully cognisant of the facts yourself – it's happened to us all from time to time.'

Lord Thorneycroft beamed at me across the table, chuckled to himself and continued with his obversations. 'She has a brilliant mind, and she possesses great mastery of detail, but what she has developed now, which is more important than an aptitude for detail, is an ability to see the main objectives. It's a mistake for a Prime Minister to become too absorbed with detail. It's important for them to see the main themes, the great sweep of possibilities ahead and to try and steer the strategy as well as the tactics, and in my view, Margaret is thinking more and more about the long-term position.'

Teddy Taylor, who lost his seat at Cathcart, Glasgow, in May 1979 and was subsequently elected as MP for Southend-on-Sea in March 1980, commented: 'Margaret Thatcher drives herself immensely hard. Her standards are immensely high and she makes sure that we all work very hard. She's a difficult person to work for because she does demand extremely high standards from all those around her. If you're trying to present a case and if your arguments haven't been carefully thought out she will lose no opportunity in making it quite plain to you that you haven't measured up to the required standards. She is a very delightful person and a charming person, but there's no way you can just drift along with Maggie.'

'While she is extraordinarily hard working, I don't think I have ever heard her comment on how hard anybody else works; she leaves that very much to them. Nevertheless, she does expect results. After all, some people work faster than others; but you are certainly expected to know what you are talking about – how long you took to reach your conclusion is up to you. I have observed one thing about her, though, which I find very much to her credit. I've noticed particularly since she became Prime Minister that when something goes wrong, as it inevitably does from time to time, she doesn't dwell upon it. She tends to say "Well, we could have done that one better, now what do we do?" She doesn't harp back on past errors. She goes forward all the time, which is very refreshing. It's *too* exhausting to rake over all the mistakes which all of us make all of the time.'

He hesitated, looked thoughtful for a moment and smiled. 'On the whole she's a woman I prefer not to make too many mistakes in front of. She is always very kind to me but it's preferable not to make too many.'

It should also be said that despite the immense and unremitting pressures upon her, if you're in any kind of trouble it's as if she had dropped everything to help you, to care for you, which is really quite remarkable considering the virtually overwhelming demands upon her time. Her capacity for compassion in cases of individual misfortune is very great indeed.'

Many observers have contended that Margaret Thatcher's background and upbringing have had a profound influence on her political philosophy. Several critics have claimed that she admires only those people who have

125

pulled themselves up by their own bootlaces. Adam Raphael, writing in *The Observer,* expressed the opinion that 'Mrs Thatcher's views on race, social security, capital punishment and a whole range of other social issues, are not only distinct from those of her predecessors but distasteful to many of her more aristocratic colleagues.'

Did Lord Thorneycroft concur with that view?

'Yes, I think that's probably true. I must say it's rather difficult to talk about capital punishment and social security in the same context. I think I would treat capital punishment and social security in a slightly different bracket: it's not easy to fit such diverse topics into the same reply. Anyway I would dismiss capital punishment; after all, everyone has different views on that issue and those views are nothing whatsoever to do with social security. As far as social security is concerned I think she was brought up in a background where however humble your circumstances you were expected to do your very best to look after yourself and your family – that was the first line of defence. If other people helped, well and good, but the first line of defence was yourself, your parents, your children and your family. You were all a unit and you tried to do the very best you could for one another.

'I don't think she has ever lost that approach to life. I think she still feels it very strongly. In my view, she feels that to some degree we have lost that attitude of mind, lost it perhaps for the best reasons in a desire to be kind and good to people, but somehow it's taken away their sense of responsibility and independence. It's my belief that she likes to feel for a situation in which people who really are poor or unfortunate or sick are always looked after, are always cared for, but where the great mass of people look to themselves to be their own first security. I think that is her attitude. Now it may be said that such a viewpoint differs from other people in public life. It certainly differs from the attitude of most of the British people over the last fifteen or twenty years. They haven't subscribed to that view, but she does, passionately. Well, if it's new, it's refreshing, and it may be right. The comment in *The*

126

Observer is fair. It's a new idea, a new approach.'

It is conceded that the premiership of Margaret Thatcher heralded a new standpoint on one of the most contentious issues in British politics today, namely the role of the Welfare State and its various ramifications. However, the philosophy of any political party has to address itself to an ever increasing range of domestic and world affairs. As previously quoted, Margaret Thatcher is reputed to have stated 'I have changed everything.' How did Lord Thorneycroft interpret that response? Had she instigated a change in Conservative philosophy. Had she indeed changed everything?

'Well, no. I think people can read too much into an answer. In a way it's absolutely true to say that every Prime Minister changes everything because a totally new pattern of approach is adopted – that's undoubtedly true. However, I think Margaret Thatcher would probably hotly deny any suggestion that she was out of the main trend of Conservative philosophy. In fact she might as well say there were others who were trying to get rather further away from the broad trend of Conservative philosophy and that she herself was more of an original Conservative, believing in the native worth and goodness of people, believing that if you give them independence and freedom and responsibility, on the whole you get a better set of decisions than is the case when you delegate the role of decision-making to a wise bunch of civil servants. In other words she believes that people should determine their own destiny, shape their own lives, make their own decisions, that it is not the proper function of the Civil Service to take those decisions for them. So if by saying "I have changed everything" she meant that she was going to let people have a bash at it themselves, then I think that's absolutely true. However, it's easy to exaggerate the position. She hasn't wound up the social services. She hasn't abolished free education or done anything of that nature. She is keeping up a trend of social services in this country which has been common under Conservative, Labour and Liberal Parties. It is simply that she doesn't want to lose

127

the individuality of individual people.'

It has been alleged that unlike her predecessors, Margaret Thatcher has not sought to build up a strong personal staff, that in comparison with past Prime Ministers she is somewhat isolated.

'In my opinion,' says Lord Thorneycroft, 'she has rather a good staff: I never quite know what people mean by "personal staff" but if you're thinking in terms of numbers I don't think she believes that numbers help very much – she's rather an un-numbers person. I think that Margaret demands quality rather than quantity in her advisors, but while she has high-quality advisors around her, I have observed since she became Prime Minister that she takes great trouble to invite small groups of people to lunch or to a meeting, and encourages them to talk very freely to her. She listens very attentively to their views, and in that kind of relaxed atmosphere the best advice is often proffered.'

Downing Street was constructed by Sir George Downing (1624–84), an English diplomat and public servant who made vigorous contributions to his country's prosperity as a financial and commercial administrator. During his lifetime he amassed a great fortune and was reputed to be one of the richest men in England.

In 1735, Sir Robert Walpole became the first premier to occupy No 10 as the official residence of the Prime Minister, but after nearly two and half centuries that unchallenged male preserve has its first female tenant. 'We've never had an animal quite like her before,' remarked Lord Pannell, and one is reminded of the anguished cry of 'Why can't a woman be more like a man?' from Professor Higgins. But after the initial novelty has worn off, does the fact that the new tenant is female really make any difference to the everyday happenings at No 10?

'Well, they're not like us, do you know what I mean?' He peered at me quizzically. 'The fact that she was a woman made a difference in the election but I say that both ways – it counted for much in both directions. There was a lot of talk about her being a woman, and in my view

Right: Chairman Hua, of the Chinese Republic, leaves London after a meeting with Mrs Thatcher; *below:* a Common Market problem during Mrs Thatcher's meeting with Italian Prime Minister Signor Cossiga early in 1980

Left: talking with a delegate at the International Year of Child Young People's Parliament, County Hall; *below:* the critical female eye in action at local women's shop in Milton Keynes, where Mrs Thatcher opened shopping centre

if she had lost it would have very difficult to get another woman elected as Party Leader. Everybody would have blamed her defeat, at least to some extent, on the fact that she was a woman: I don't feel there's any doubt about that. But now that she is Prime Minister I don't think it really matters a damn. Next time I don't think she will be judged on whether she's a woman at all. At the next election she will be judged on what she has done, on her performance not as a woman but as a Prime Minister.'

Lord Thorneycroft reflected for a moment. 'It's important though to recognise that she is a woman. They're not like us and it's no good pretending that they are: Margaret really is a feminine person with feminine instincts, quick reactions, application to detail and all manner of characteristics which are much more developed in a woman than they are in a man. She has all those feminine attributes which are undoubtedly important attributes – and they're conspicuous – but the total result is an extremely effective human being.'

Even the most ardent cynic would find it impossible to describe Margaret Thatcher as 'negative'. She is a forceful personality who inspires wrath in her adversaries and adulation in her supporters. She has been variously described as 'the axe woman', a hard-line élitist, Boadicea and Joan of Arc and it would undoubtedly appear that she evokes more heartfelt reaction than other leading political figures.

'That's true, I think people do have very definite views on her. People probably do react to her in a rather more positive way than is the case with other politicians. To make a study of her, you really ought to look abroad. The Japanese were telling me that at the Tokyo summit the one person they wished to see of all the world leaders was Margaret Thatcher. When she was in New York thousands of people were trying to hire planes to fly in from all over that vast continent to listen to her speak. She really is a fascinating phenomenon!'

Does the Prime Minister get noticeably depressed by the gloomy forecasts which emanate from the Treasury from time to time: by the prophets of doom who confidently predict that nothing can save Britain from economic disaster?

'She's not oblivious to the blows of fortune. If you come down to breakfast and find you've sunk another four points in the polls, I've always thought she must feel bloody awful. She's human and she obviously does get depressed, but she doesn't either conceal the fact that she's feeling depressed nor allow it to interfere with her work. She gets straight on with the job!'

The Opposition Parties, trade union leaders and even some 'faint-hearted' Tories allege that the Government will eventually be forced into making U-turns, particularly on various aspects of their economic policy. Was that a real prospect?

'I think you have to be rather careful when talking about "U" turns. If you develop such a phobia about U-turns with the result that you are fearful of changing anything, then I think you are in danger of becoming frenetic on the subject. People do instigate certain changes, they do adjust a bit here and a bit there. Nevertheless, I don't think she is going to start doing U-turns on the main themes of her policy – no! If she thinks we are spending too much money, you'll find we will spend less. If we are employing too many civil servants you'll find we will employ fewer – she won't make any changes on those aspects of her policy. In my opinion, if she sees some great hardship somewhere, somebody who is being rather knocked about by a particular policy, she is quite capable of stepping in and saying "Don't go so fast there." She's a woman of common-sense, but she won't change course. No, definitely not!'

The Prime Minister's opponents claim that she will inexorably pursue her hard-line policies with ruthless determination, irrespective of their unpopularity, and irrespective of the feelings of the electorate.

'She's a politician, you must remember that; she's a politician and the art of politics is, as Ram said, "the art of the possible". She won't go wildly ahead of public opinion so as to lose all their support and secure the defeat of her Party. She might see her Party defeated but not deliberately in pursuit of some aim which proved to be practically unsalable. She won't do that. She is a skilled professional and the art of the skilled professional is to carry public opinion with you, to be, wherever possible, ahead of public opinion. To identify public opinion when it is brave and when everybody else says it is fearful – she has a gift for that. But it doesn't mean she will implement policies which everybody will condemn because you can't govern a country that way. You have to govern a country by persuasion, by encouragement, by urging it into greater activity and by showing courage yourself. She's not indifferent to public opinion but she's prepared to lead public opinion.

'She is perfectly prepared to start debates on unmentionable subjects. They used to say of her that she had the most unfortunate habit of actually saying what she thought and this was considered a very novel and dangerous innovation in public life. Now she has a habit of doing what she says, which is even more startling! She is a very courageous woman, but she is a professional politician and if people are sitting around waiting, in the hope that she'll fall flat on her face, I think they are going to be sorely disappointed. She moves with caution. She undoubtedly possesses something which people were looking for: she voices the views which perhaps lay unexpressed within many people's minds. But don't underestimate the sheer professionalism that she has. She's a very astute politician.'

Brian Walden considered Margaret Thatcher to be 'a very good leader of the Opposition, the best Tory leader of the Opposition he had ever seen'. But how did Lord Thorneycroft assess her performance in the more formidable and responsible role of Prime Minister?

'She is much better as Prime Minister than she was as Leader of the Opposition. She fits much more easily into the role of Prime Minister, which is just as well because that's what the country needs.

'As Prime Minister, she's more capable of decentralizing; she takes rather a longer view; she's rather more unruffled

131

when things go wrong; she's more of a statesman. The role of Prime Minister is by far the harder one to fill, but she actually fills it the better of the two.

'Margaret will certainly adhere to her main beliefs. She will certainly hold fast to the main strategy, but politics is more than sticking to beliefs and strategy. There are other factors that are important: dealing with crisis management of every kind and on every scale, dealing with a world which is constantly changing all around you – and remember many of the things which happen are entirely beyond your control – they require *enormous* patience and skill and she is developing those qualities all the time.

'She will undoubtedly hold onto the course that she has set herself, but the test of a Prime Minister is more than holding onto a course, for many of them have a vision of the direction they want to take. The test of a Prime Minister is to be able to ride the storm, to be able to deal with the desperate gales which swing in on your flank and yet still cling on to the intended course. Everybody goes through bad patches; she is bound to have the most frightful rough ride but she will still hold on. She won't panic.

'I personally believe she will do it, that she will succeed, but time will have to prove her success.'

Lord Home – 'People know what she is going to do. I think this is her great asset.'

Alexander Frederick Douglas Home is the eldest son of the thirteenth Earl of Home. The title Earl of Home had been held since 1605 by members of the famous border family of Home, whose ancestral stronghold was Home Castle in Berwickshire and who claim descent from the great comital house of Dunbar. His mother was the daughter of the fourth Earl of Durham and he was educated at Eton and Christ Church, Oxford.

Lord Home's aristocratic titles have a musical-chair quality. Earl of Home, of course, was a hereditary title which he disclaimed in 1963 to become a mere 'Sir Alec', a title which, in fact, allowed him to become one of the few genuinely aristocratic Prime Ministers of the past few decades. In 1974 this cycle was completed when he returned to the House of Lords bearing the title Home of the Hirsel.

Lord Home greeted me with all the old world charm and courtesy that one would expect from such a gentleman. He eyed my tape recorder with a nervous smile. 'There's very little I can tell you I'm afraid.' He looked decidedly uncomfortable in the role of interviewee and I can only liken his appearance to a man who manages to look guilty at the customs when in fact he genuinely has nothing to declare. I did my best to put him at his ease. Lord Home is a braces man, and the braces were much in evidence. His thumbs planted resolutely behind them, he flexed them till they rebounded with a loud thwack against his chest. He must have been black and blue and we hadn't even started the interview.

'I was originally MP for South Lanark and saw a lot of Government posts. I was in the Scottish Office as Minister of State for four years, then I was appointed to the Commonwealth Office and in 1957 I became Leader of The House of Lords and Lord President of the Council. I was Foreign Secretary twice, serving in the Cabinets of both Harold MacMillan and Ted Heath and it was the office I particularly enjoyed because it involved dealing with people all the time, which is what I really like doing.'

Did you enjoy the premiership?

'I didn't spend long enough at No 10 to know whether I enjoyed it or not. It was only a year which was an electioneering year. Being the last year of Parliament there wasn't any legislation left to carry out. It was simply a question of preparing for an election which we lost by a short head.'

In 1963 Lord Home reached the peak of his career when

133

he succeeded Harold MacMillan to the office of Prime Minister. To what extent was he aware of the lady who only four years before had taken her seat on the back-benches, the lady who was ultimately destined to occupy a unique place in British history?

'Of course, I knew her as a member of Parliament but not very well, I only really came into contact with her when she went to the Ministry of Education. At that time I was particularly impressed by her degree of competence. When she had to describe what her policy was going to be or what she would like it to be, she did so in the clearest terms so that you couldn't possibly mistake her purpose.

'Since then, of course, she has had much more practice in public. She quite clearly believes in telling the country what her policy is, and she has become very skilled in that sphere. People know what she is going to do. I think this is her great asset. As Prime Minister, she has the best opportunity of all the ministers to advertise Government policy and explain its aims.

'I think she does that very clearly and simply and leaves her audience in no doubt. There's a lot to be said for that – it's really what leadership is all about right or wrong.'

Drawing from your own experiences as PM, which personal attributes do you feel are particularly necessary to enable you to withstand the intense pressures of such a responsible office?

'The one thing a Prime Minister has to do is to take the decisions and he always finds that other people are very reluctant to do so, therefore the ability to decide is really an essential prerequisite in a Prime Minister. Clearly, too, Mrs Thatcher has that ability. She has very difficult issues to deal with, probably more complex on the economic side than they have been for a very long time in this country, but everybody is fully aware of her strategy.

'What you have to look for in her, as indeed you do in any other Prime Minister, is whether she has the authority that goes with leadership. Margaret Thatcher undoubtedly possesses that air of authority.

'Patience is another factor. While patience is a quality which every public figure should possess, this particularly applies to the office of Prime Minister, because everything comes to you as PM and you're constantly dealing with all sorts of people on all sorts of difficult issues. I don't know that there are any other particular qualifications. The main thing is to be yourself – and again I don't think that anybody can doubt that she is!'

Is the role of Prime Minister a very lonely one?

'Well, in one way it's lonely because you're exposed when you have to take the decisions; that is the job which only the PM can do. On the other hand you have a Cabinet and you have a thousand and one people wanting to see you every day, so in that sense it's not lonely at all. It's simply lonely because there is no one else to take the decisions.'

Before the election, Teddy Taylor commented: 'One of the characteristics I particularly admire about Margaret Thatcher is her genuine concern not to get out of touch. She takes every opportunity she can to talk to people about their ideas, their hopes and their fears, and one of her great strengths is that she takes their views seriously. She differs from most other leading politicians in that she is just as interested in the views of a factory worker as she is in the views of her Deputy Leader.' But it is widely acknowledged that the more exalted your position the more remote you are likely to become from grass roots opinion. Looking back on your year in office, do the constant calls upon a Prime Minister's time make the task of keeping in touch with public opinion particularly difficult?

'The difficulty is that you are so busy; there's such a pressure of engagements that it's rather difficult, firstly, to be in The House of Commons as much as you ought to be and, secondly, to keep in touch with the Party. Your private secretary naturally tries to keep your diary as free as he can because the trouble with the office of Prime Minister is that all sorts of issues constantly arise, which haven't been anticipated, probably couldn't be anticipated. There's a lot of people to see in the international field as well,

135

particularly now we're members of the European Community. But Margaret has very good advisors; Lord Thorneycroft is a very good Chairman of the Party, and I'm sure she manages to keep in touch, but there's no doubt it is difficult – yes – much more difficult than it is for any other minister, with the possible exception of The Foreign Secretary.'

Margaret Thatcher is a 'conviction politician'. How difficult is it to put your own deep-felt convictions into practice once you become Prime Minister?

'First of all, you have to carry your departmental Minister with you – whoever is most concerned with any particular issue – then you have to carry the Cabinet. Consequently, any PM may have to modify his views to some extent, but undoubtedly, a Prime Minister does set the theme and the pace.'

To what extent are you the prisoner of the views of your Cabinet?

'You can't really talk about it in terms of being a prisoner. A collective decision is taken, led by the Prime Minister or the minister who wants to carry out a particular policy—but you work as a team.'

For the sake of supposition, if the views of the Prime Minister are diametrically opposed to those of the Cabinet, who in the final analysis would win the day?

'Well, I think whenever you come up against a situation like that you're faced with resignations, aren't you? But that kind of problem very seldom arises. Over the forty years plus that I've been in Parliament I think there have only been about four cases of resignation, which is minimal compared with all the Parliamentary business implemented throughout the years.

'If a Prime Minister wanted to carry out a particular policy he would first ask the Minister concerned for his opinions, then there would be all sorts of papers circulating giving the advantages and disadvantages – it's a process of discussion and decision. Either the Prime Minister or the minister concerned may start with a preconceived idea but may change it or modify it in some way, so that eventually

136

you get the right answer. But it's a collective decision.

'If a Prime Minister can't do certain things because of the views of the Cabinet, then it's probable that your views ought to be modified anyhow, so you accept that. But it doesn't arise. As I say, four or five resignations when you consider all the major issues there have been over the last forty years is infinitesimal really.'

To what extent are a Government's actions subject to the dictates of Whitehall?

'You listen to the Civil Service, but the job of a politician is to make up his own mind. The function of a civil servant is to give the minister, as honestly as he can, both sides of the argument, or even three sides if there are three sides. But there is a clear distinction. It is for the Minister to take the decisions.'

While the function of a minister and a civil servant is clearly designated, it is frequently said that the Civil Service, though not an elected body, wields a disproportionate amount of power behind the scenes. How powerful is the Civil Service? Can it frustrate the will of the Prime Minister?

'No, it can't; that's the wrong premise – it can't. Of course the Prime Minister can *let* her will be frustrated, but that's very unlikely,' chortled Lord Home, throwing me a meaningful glance. 'The Prime Minister is there to decide. As I say, the function of the Civil Service is quite clear. I've worked with them for years and years and years and they don't exceed their function – they give balanced arguments.'

Does the Prime Minister, or the minister concerned, often find it necessary to over-rule the Civil Service?

'It's not a question of over-ruling; that's where some journalists go wrong. It's a question of the Prime Minister or minister being given the pros and cons. It's for the politician, to decide whether the pros or cons win. A civil servant doesn't feel himself over-ruled. He has done his job and accepts and works with whatever policy is decided.'

Ever since Margaret Thatcher won the leadership in 1975, the Opposition have claimed that her particular

137

brand of Conservatism represented a departure from traditional Tory philosophy. It has been claimed that she is a hard-line Right-Winger whose views are totally distinct from other post-war Conservative Prime Ministers and whose leadership marks a new era in British politics.

'I know a lot of people say she's to the right of the Party, but I think these labels are rather facile. Because she happens personally to be in favour of the death penalty she's labelled 'Right Wing', but there are an awful lot of other people in favour of the death penalty who couldn't possibly be labelled 'Right'. I think it's too easy to attach these labels to people. Incidentally, the death penalty isn't a bad example of how you have to modify your own point of view. She could have had a vote on it in the House of Commons, a Party vote, but she left it without a Whip. Consequently, it's quite a good example of the way a Prime Minister doesn't necessarily get her way.

'Margaret Thatcher gives her version of Conservative policies but I don't know where I would place them in relation to the "centre". They seem to me to be eminently sensible! There is always a difference of opinion on any economic policy – always. If it's the policies of Professor Friedman which Mrs Thatcher chooses to favour they would say they were "Right Wing" policies, but if they are *right,* if they work out in practice, I don't think it matters if they are "Right Wing or Left Wing".

'Again, I don't think she has changed the traditional Conservative approach. I think what she has done is to change the economic direction – the direction of economic policy – and by and large this fits in with a good many Conservative interpretations, that the State should interfere in the *minimum* way – that the intervention of the State in industry should be kept to a minimum. In that sense she has changed a lot, but while that is undoubtedly a change, it's not necessarily a change in Conservative philosophy.

'We have always aimed to tread that path, but, in post-war years it's been extremely difficult to keep the State out of it. In fact the State is right in it now, of course, and this is where the difficulties arise in industries like steel, electricity and coal. It's a big operation to reverse the progress of the Socialist State, but there's a great deal of sympathy for doing it. The Government is a huge employer, you can't get away from that, but she has changed a lot . . . yes!'

Lord Home was born into the aristocracy. How did he view the allegation that Margaret Thatcher's views on a whole host of issues ranging from social security to capital punishment were both distinct from those of her predecessors and distasteful to many of her more aristocratic Cabinet colleagues?

'Nonsense! Her opinions are distinct but it has nothing to do with her more aristocratic colleagues so far as I am aware. Nonsense!' With that Lord Home emitted an aristocratic guffaw, punctuated by a further thwack of the braces.

Common rumour or gossip profoundly influences the conclusions of many people. In the 1979 General Election only nineteen women candidates were elected to serve as Members of Parliament and the House of Commons still remains an essentially male-dominated forum. Does the fact that much of the Parliamentary gossip takes place within the walls of men-only clubs such as Bucks and Whites create certain difficulties for the present Prime Minister?

'Yes, it is rather more difficult for a woman Prime Minister – that's undoubtedly true. On the other hand, she has PPSs, and it's their job to keep the PM in touch with general opinion. I've had personal experience of that office because at one time I was a PPS, but Prime Ministers are very busy – even male PMs haven't much time to go to places like Bucks or Whites or wherever you pick up all the gossip. You do rely quite extensively on your PPS to tell you what the groundswells in the Party are.'

It is frequently said that Margaret Thatcher's style of leadership is in direct contrast to both pre-war and post-war Conservative Prime Ministers.

'All these comparisons are odious. In my view, every Prime Minister is different from the other. She is a very powerful, direct leader of opinion on her own merit – there's no doubt about that! I think it's true to say that she is launching a crusade to try to stop the rot in this country. We've been gradually going downhill for a number of reasons; in my opinion the trade unions are very much bound up in those reasons as a result of the kind of advice they have been giving to their rank and file over a number of years. Consequently, I think it is extremely valuable that she has come out very strongly in favour of the freedom of the rank and file trade unionist, that she champions their freedom in just the same way as she champions the freedom of each and every other individual in our society. She's quite right! Power goes to people's heads. It always has throughout the whole of history – the kings, the Church, the barons, the monopolies – now you've got the trade unions and power can mislead them.'

A Prime Minister is constantly obliged to take harsh decisions; accordingly popularity may be a transient phenomenum. How important is it for a Prime Minister to be liked by the electorate?

'I don't think you need necessarily be "liked" I think you have to be respected. Popularity is rather temporary, isn't it? If you do something of which people disapprove,' said Lord Home with a wry smile, 'they cease to like you, at least for the time being. You may ultimately recapture their favour, but the important factor is *respect*. As long as you are respected for what you do, that's really all you can ever hope for.'

How important is it to form your Cabinet from people who subscribe to your own views, whose convictions are your convictions and whose commitments are your commitments?

'You obviously want people in your Cabinet who are committed to the main theme of the policy. Short of that, you simply don't know what their views will be on any particular issue before you take office, though you may have some idea. As you work as a team, you don't deliberately choose somebody who is out on a limb – if you're sure he's out on a limb. You certainly don't go out of your way to do that.

'The Cabinet should be broadly representative of all

sections of the Party but you have to choose people on their merits and on the public form they have previously displayed. The Party knows them pretty well, people are inclined to think of a Cabinet suddenly emerging – but it doesn't. People have been junior ministers, they have come up through the Party, they have made their speeches at Party conferences and they have come right up through the Party machine, so you know the form pretty well. They are rather like racehorses really – they've been exposed. It doesn't always work but it is a good guide.'

When the storm clouds gather overhead as they frequently do in the lifetime of a Parliament, how difficult is it for a Prime Minister to hold to the course, to keep to the main strategy, especially if some members of the Cabinet and indeed backbenchers publicly express a degree of scepticism and doubt about the merits of some of the Governments's major policies?

'I don't think that it is difficult. Sometimes, of course, you have some difficulty with colleagues but again it's an example of how over the whole field of politics a Prime Minister is constantly modifying an opinion, or you get a compromise solution and there is nothing wrong in the word "compromise". A compromise solution can be a very sensible solution, indeed the most sensible solution, so I don't think this difficulty really arises, but it can – it can in limited circumstances.

'U-turn is another label – a shorthand description of events. I don't think people often make U-turns, though I suppose you can cite certain events and classify them as such. Regarding the wages and incomes legislation, we pursued that for some time to see if it was practical. Both Socialist and Conservative Governments were turned down by the respective Parliaments on a wages and incomes policy and I suppose you can say it's a U-turn if you embark upon another course, but it's simply a reaction to events which have proved the policy to be unworkable.

'I say again, U-turns don't often happen. If they do, it's really more a matter of reaction to public opinion and to experience than anything else. You may get bumped off a

141

policy because it simply doesn't work and Parliament won't have it – you had a case in the last Parliament on the Devolution Bill – the Labour Government had to drop that.'

It is generally accepted that Margaret Thatcher's election to the leadership of the Tory Party was in part an accident brought about by a particular set of circumstances. As a former Prime Minister, knowing the demands and pitfalls of that office, you are in a unique position to adjudicate upon her election.

'In my view, Margaret Thatcher was the right choice as Leader. The situation was made for her very direct approach to politics, people recognised that and elected her. She coincided with a mood in the country which was right for somebody of her kind of active and strong point of view. I think she was a very good choice indeed.

'I think she will be a success, too. She has the quality of directness, the quality of clear-sightedness and the quality which enables her to take decisions. In addition, she's technically very well accomplished. She is also full of human sympathy for all the problems people face. From her own experiences she knows how difficult life can be and she hasn't changed in herself since becoming Prime Minister – she has always been a very nice person. I hope she knows the answers to our economic problems – no one has up to now, so I hope she will solve them.'

The interview at an end, Lord Home rose courteously and smiled. 'I hope you'll excuse me, I have a luncheon appointment.' With a final thwack of his braces and a relieved sigh, he made his way to the Lords' dining room.

Sir Keith Joseph – 'She's a vigorous character . . . she inspires a healthy respect.'

'My political career has been immensely long. I've been in politics twenty-four years and the country has been going downhill ever since,' remarked Sir Keith with a wry grin.

The Right Honourable Sir Keith Joseph has been MP for Leeds North East since 1956. He served in the 1939–45 war as a captain in the Royal Artillery and was wounded in the Italian campaign and mentioned in despatches. 'I've been in four Conservative cabinets under four Conservative Prime Ministers and I've tried to learn from mistakes, including my mistakes.' Sir Keith has held several key positions including Minister of State at the Board of Trade, Minister for Housing and Local Government and Minister for Welsh Affairs under both Sir Harold MacMillan and Sir Alec Douglas Home. He was Secretary of State for Social Services under Ted Heath between 1970–74 and in May 1979 Margaret Thatcher appointed him to the highly sensitive position of Secretary of State for Industry.

Sir Keith occupies an office on the eleventh floor of the imposing Department of Industry building in Victoria. The room is spacious with picture windows, a large, well-used desk and a small comfortable settee.

The higher echelons of politics is not a forum for the faint-hearted; as Margaret Thatcher has commented, 'If you are in politics, you must not be super-sensitive.' Sir Keith would have to agree. He has been subjected to more diatribes and invective at the hands of his opponents than any senior politician can reasonably expect. He has been variously described as Rasputin, the mad monk, the Ayatolla and an extremist right-wing hardliner who threatens the very fabric of our society.

The moment I entered the room Sir Keith jumped to his

feet and greeted me with a warm reassuring smile. As he ushered me towards the comfortable chair, his brow furrowed; 'I don't think I can be of much help to you. I'm not very good at this sort of thing. I'm not a journalist – I don't think I know any useful anecdotes – oh dear!'

Sir Keith is a very shy, gentle man with an infectious laugh and a dry sense of humour. Clearly the way he is portrayed by some of his more vociferous opponents bears no resemblance at all to the man in question. As the interview progressed, it became increasingly apparent that he is a man of great emotion with an overwhelming desire to see this country regain some of its past greatness.

His first encounter with Margaret Thatcher was when she made her début in Parliament in 1959. 'Over the years we have worked on various policy groups together and in 1970–74 we both served in the Cabinet under Ted Heath. After the first 1974 election, we formed the Centre for Policy Studies because we were both very keen to re-establish the understanding – re-establish may be too hopeful a word – to strengthen the understanding of what we call the social market economy: that is to say the market economy within a humane framework of laws, institutions and safety-nets. This Centre for Policy Studies of which we were the founder members is still in existence today.'

Had he envisaged Margaret Thatcher as a potential leader? The prospect of a woman at the helm of the Conservative Party may have been too radical a concept for the early sixties.

'It wasn't at all difficult to identify her as a potentially outstanding Conservative politician from very early on. Her combination of clear head, warm heart, powerful energy and great patriotism distinguished her from the beginning. But it wasn't until after the October 1974 election that one began to consider possibilities for the future.'

And then?

'She was chosen by a substantial majority on the usual basis that people get chosen, because on balance they're preferred over the alternatives. Each person who voted for her in that leadership election saw in her, no doubt, a different combination of advantages. I can only speak for myself and tell you what I saw in her. I saw in her, overwhelmingly, the strongest combination of required attributes which embodied qualities of head and heart, and above all guts!' This reference to 'guts' was uttered with great emotion; he paused for a moment and continued. 'Head, heart, guts and passion for her country. Now all the others had these to some extent, obviously all the others had these. It wasn't as if some of them had none of these things. They all had them but it was the combination and the strength of these attributes in her which was the overriding factor.'

Emphasising the word 'courage', even Margaret Thatcher's fiercest critics and opponents would acknowledge that she has infinite reserves of true valour – 'She is a born fighter' is an oft-heard remark.

Sir Keith agrees.

'The key factor is that she has moral courage. There are many men of great physical courage, great physical courage, who do not necessarily have political courage. I'm not making comments on individual colleagues, of course, but personally I know she has more moral courage than I have, though I don't say that's a great measure.'

'The word courage is sometimes misunderstood. What we're talking about in this case is not physical courage; any woman who has children has courage – that's a man's point of view perhaps – but most women have great courage. I'm specifically referring to Margaret's moral courage under public exposure – very, very public exposure indeed.'

Prior to the election, but more particularly during the campaign itself, political adversaries and trade union leaders constantly referred to Margaret Thatcher and Sir Keith Joseph as if they were an indivisible unit. Their names were continually linked together. When I mentioned it a look of anger mingled with a certain sadness flashed across Sir Keith's face:

'Only by opponents, because they wanted to smear *her* with me! I was considered a bogey, so I was used as a stick

145

with which to beat her. Yes, it was all good tactics, a ploy by the Opposition.'

But how closely did his views coincide with hers? Sir Keith contemplated the question for several moments.

'Well, that's more for her to say than for me. Anyway, I was used as a stick with which to beat her by opponents. However, I certainly share her views,' he said softly.

According to Greek legend, Mentor was the adviser of Telemachus, hence the modern usage for sage adviser. Throughout history, those who achieve fame and those for whom destiny has chosen a more inconspicuous role have frequently stressed the need for a mentor. Did Margaret Thatcher share that need? Did she have a mentor?

Sir Keith chuckled to himself, 'I should think she has dozens in the sense that she learns. She's a learner. Some people stop learning, but she's learning the whole while. In stressing this, I'm saying something which to my mind is very creditable, full of praise. She's always learning and she's had to learn a great deal. Experience is a mentor for her. Books are a mentor for her. The past is a mentor for her; she is to some extent a student of history. She respects learning, historical learning, and she respects the views and opinions of all sorts of living human beings from all sorts of backgrounds, from far outside politics including her own family background; and added to this are all the lessons from her own life experience. They are all, as it were, contributions to her, but I don't know of any single individual, certainly not myself, who could possibly be described individually as a mentor – no.

'She might say that Lord Hailsham is somebody to whose word she always listens with great respect; I think she probably would, but that's for her to say, not for me. However, apart from a very senior and immensely experienced old warrior such as he, I don't think it's appropriate to talk of a mentor. She's a learner!'

Patrick Cosgrave, in his biography of Margaret Thatcher, recounted the question he posed to her in 1976 just one year after she had been elected Leader of the Conservative Party: 'I asked her what she thought she had

146

changed since becoming Leader. "I have changed everything," she said simply.' Did Sir Keith agree with that contention? Did he feel this was a justifiable claim?

Sir Keith slowly sipped his tea before replying carefully. 'She happened to coincide with a time when the old ideas, the shared perceptions, had been shown to have failed. And she was brave enough in terms of moral courage to recognise they had failed, and ready to shift the centre of argument towards a new approach in a number of fields. She was perhaps particularly keen to re-establish the old Conservative priorities of patriotism, defence, law and order, all on a sound base of education and economic housekeeping. But I think it was the readiness to recognise that the old ideas had failed that led to the claim of "having changed everything". Yes, she's changed the whole basis of the argument.'

A momentary glimpse of the spontaneous reactions of those in public life may provide a rare insight into their personality; such a moment was captured by Adam Raphael in *The Observer*: 'There is no doubt that she inspires a healthy apprehension among her ministers. Mr Jim Prior, the Employment Secretary, recently came out of her office in No 10 to find Sir Keith Joseph waiting his turn. "Don't worry, Keith," joked Prior, "I have roughed her up good and proper." "Oh Lord, have you?" said Sir Keith, pressing a worried hand to his brow, "I was hoping to get her agreement today." Sir Keith's complexion visibly reddened with the utterance of almost every word, and as his blushes grew deeper the sound of his laughter rippled through the air. "She's a vigorous character. She never fails to put a point of view very strongly. God bless her . . . thank the Lord!" '

But does she, as claimed, inspire a healthy apprehension among her ministers?

'She inspires a healthy respect. You shouldn't even be able to expect to get away with weak arguments with any Prime Minister. She sets very high standards herself and she is widely informed. She has a very retentive memory. In fact she has an embarrassingly retentive memory,' observed Sir Keith with a chuckle, his face reddening once again as if reliving some past experience. 'And all that's fine, I wouldn't wish it otherwise.' Still chuckling, he continued, 'She will remember what someone said even if it was a long time ago or what she read in a newspaper or periodical. Yes, she has a very capacious memory – a good mental filing system.'

'Funnily enough, I said to her recently, is it harder than it was in Opposition, is it more work? Speaking for myself, I don't find it any harder in Government; in a way, being in the Shadow Cabinet was harder because when you're in Opposition you don't get any help. You don't have, as I have now, very able and nice people assisting you; you have to do it all yourself. For example, I have a driver paid for by you, a car paid for by you – yes, Opposition is very heavy work. But enough of me. Margaret said it was no more arduous being PM than it was being Leader of the Opposition.'

Every Prime Minister has brought to that office his own distinctive style of leadership, but it has been said that the premiership of Margaret Thatcher marks a break with the past, that her style of leadership is radically different from that of her predecessors. Did Sir Keith feel that her 'style' was fundamentally different?

'Well yes, but they all differ from one another, don't they? However, I can't call to mind any particular facet of her leadership that sets her quite apart from her predecessors.'

He refrained from any further comment on that issue and continued, 'She has had a wide range of interests. She shadowed the Treasury, and her experience in Opposition and in Government has been relatively wide, though it hadn't embraced the foreign side. It's in the sphere of foreign affairs that she has had to acquire experience both as Leader of the Opposition and as Prime Minister and I think it's widely acknowledged that she has learnt a very great deal and very fast. On a personal level, she has always made herself particularly approachable to backbenchers, particularly approachable, and she has continued in that vein as Prime Minister.'

More approachable than her predecessor?

'Yes, I think that's true. I think she is again learning. I think she perceived that Ted Heath, with his own particular manifestations of public service, had one set of priorities and she was aware of the comments that he was relatively inaccessible to backbenchers. Margaret has certainly made sure that no one could level that criticism at her. She is very very determined to remain aware of backbench opinion!'

While Margaret Thatcher is renowned for her strong stance on a number of vital issues, she is equally well known, according to comments volunteered from both sides of the House, for her willingness to listen to the views and perceptions of others. But how difficult is it to induce a change of mind during the all-important discussions in Cabinet?

'She undoubtedly takes a firm position. She takes very strong positions indeed, but in part in order to evoke strong argument. She doesn't want waffly argument, so she puts her case strongly and expects you to knock it down strongly, but she's perfectly persuadable – yes.'

Through relentlessly hard work and inevitable personal sacrifice, Margaret Thatcher has reached the zenith of her career. But success in whatever sphere may have a profound effect on a person's disposition and personality. Had Sir Keith over the years noticed any significant change in her character, particularly since her historic arrival at No 10?

'She hasn't changed at all since she became Prime Minister – not at all. Of course, through the years she has deepened and broadened and I've always found her intensely warm and considerate, not only to me but to other people. I think the attitude of those who serve her shows this; they glow with enthusiasm. The closer you are to her the more affectionate people appear to be towards her.'

Lord Thorneycroft expressed the view that Margaret Thatcher was much better as Prime Minister than she was as Leader of the Opposition. She was more capable of decentralising, rather more unruffled when things go wrong. Did Sir Keith concur with that judgment?

149

'Yes, I think everything Lord Thorneycroft has said is right, but don't misunderstand me when I say that in my view the task of being Prime Minister is easier than the task of being Leader of the Opposition. It's easier to do, but I don't say easier to do well. Leader of the Opposition is a ghastly job, a beastly job. You have the whole while to construct in the public mind a distinct image, a philosophy, a coherent philosophy, and your only weapon is criticism, sometimes constructive criticism, sometimes negative criticism, and it's very easy to become just a critic. You have to draw attention to yourself; you have the whole while to draw attention to yourself, it's part of the job and I must emphasise again – your only weapon is criticism. Conversely, as Prime Minister, you don't have to lift a finger for attention to be focused upon you, it arises from the office, inevitably. You are always in the centre of great decisions and great events. You are indispensable. The task of projecting yourself is spontaneous and natural; it comes naturally, it doesn't have to be forced. As PM you have a great machine broadly responding to your priorities, but in Opposition it all has to be done by you. No, Leader of the Opposition is a dog's job. It's a crucial constitutional function and you appreciate its value when you go to a country like America and see that they don't have that kind of constitution, with the result that they do not have any alternative Government with a coherent alternative philosophy ready to put into practice. It's a great invention, the Leader of Her Majesty's Loyal Opposition, but it's a very heavy burden to carry – iniative, improvisation, statesmanship, all has to be conjured out of nothing, whereas the role of Prime Minister is constantly giving you material, actually *giving* you material to which you have to respond. I think Lord Thorneycroft's perception is precisely right. She was a good Leader of the Opposition but she's an even better Prime Minister!'

He looked up. 'There's one other observation I would like to make: Margaret is delightfully feminine. Despite all the pressures . . .' His brow furrowed. 'Despite all the pressures she retains her femininity intact.'

150

Lord George-Brown – 'As a politician. . . I think in every regard she stands out as among the best I've seen.'

The political and not so political exploits of Lord George-Brown have been well chronicled for more than three decades, since, in fact, his entry into Parliament in 1945 as Labour MP for Belper, a constituency he represented until 1970 when he lost his seat to a Conservative – a result which no matter what one's political persuasion caused a genuine sadness. For this is a man who has never been mealy-mouthed, as the late Nikita Khrushchev would have been only too pleased to endorse.

Between 1960 and 1970 he was Deputy Leader of the Labour Party, serving under the Leadership of both Hugh Gaitskell and Harold Wilson. In 1966 he was made Foreign Secretary in the Wilson Government, an office he subsequently resigned in March 1968 amid a flurry of dramatic publicity. In his letter of resignation to the Prime Minister he said, 'The events of last night and the long hours of this morning have brought to a head a really serious issue which has, as you know, been troubling me for some time. It is, in short, the way this Government is run, and the manner in which we reach our decisions. You and I have discussed this more than once. I regard this general issue as much more fundamental than any particular item of policy.'

This spirited and forceful politician now sits in the House of Lords as a Crossbencher, owing allegiance to no one but himself. In the past few years Lord George has had his own TV chat show (the George-Brown interviews on Southern Television) and is a regular contributor to Capital Radio – the local radio station in London. During the 1979 election campaign, however, he resigned from

Capital when the powers that be insisted his broadcasts should be recorded; they also insisted that any subsequent transmissions should be scripted and that those scripts should be submitted to the Editor prior to any broadcast. Lord George refused categorically to countenance any such constraint, regarding this intrusion as a form of censorship. It was a full four months before he went behind the microphone at Capital again – and on his terms!

As a freelance political pundit, his comments, particularly in the *Sunday Express,* spare neither friend nor foe. He is one of the most regular contributors to that newspaper and some examples of his pungency can be found in these extracts which I have selected virtually at random.

Lord George had been one of the leading lights in the foundation of the Transport and General Workers Union when, referring to Moss Evans, the present leader, he wrote these words:

'He is proving to be the most expensive disaster that has ever happened to my Union. Moss Evans is not even the puppet master. He is the puppet which pulls the strings of the others in response to the jerks on its own strings.'

Jim Prior, Conservative Employment Minister, doesn't escape the firing-line either. In the same article, he refers to him in this way:'Just like Moss Evans – an expensive disaster for the nation in his present job.'

Len Murray, General Secretary of the TUC, comes in for sharp criticism in an article entitled 'I wish my grandmother could have had a talk with Len Murray'. 'There's none so blind as those who *will* not see' was a favourite admonition frequently addressed to us kids by my dour old Scottish grandmother. . . . She came clearly into my mind's eye as I read Len Murray's latest outburst at the conference of one of the printing unions a day or so ago.' Lord George then says of Mr Murray: 'The continued failure by he and his colleagues on the TUC General Council to present the position bluntly to their members at their conference can only be put down to cowardice. That disease affects other sectors of our society's leaders too.'

It was with some trepidation that I arrived at Lord

George's office in St James's Square. 'I won't be a moment, I'm just finishing an article,' the familiar face told me, managing to eye me at the same time over his glasses.

'I'm not a Tory you know,' began Lord George when he joined me in the long oak-panelled boardroom to which I had been shown. 'I'm a Social Democrat,' he affirmed, a statement he was to repeat over and over again during the course of our interview.

Margaret Thatcher's appointment to the Cabinet in 1970 coincided with the year when George Brown, to use his own expression, 'was finally kicked out of Parliament'. 'I knew Margaret when she was Minister of Education. Naturally we met on several occasions when we were both in the House and I also saw a certain amount of her before the 1979 General Election.

'I've always had a very high regard for her. I don't see people as men or as women.' He peered at me over the top of his glasses and chuckled, 'At least not in this respect! I always felt, when she was Minister of Education, that though she was a very controversial figure if she didn't wear skirts she would be regarded as a very outstanding person. I think in a way she has always been subject to quite unfair special criticism or examination just because she is a woman and that many of the things which irritate people about her as a woman wouldn't enter into the scales if she were a man. She has certain personal disadvantages, but then don't we all? One of them, of course, is the voice. However hard she tries, it does still, on occasion, come over in a very irritating way, *but* if one thinks of her as a person, as an administrator, as a politician, I think in every regard she stands out as among the best of those I've seen, certainly in the last couple of decades.'

Are there other more far-reaching factors not referable to her being the female of the species, that give rise to a perhaps inordinate amount of criticism?

'Let's be quite clear about this. To be honest, she attracts more criticism at the moment from among Tories who ought to be loyal to her than she does from the other side. I sometimes sit up in that gallery and watch them, and I

153

think what a miserable lot of sods they are. They almost seem to be wishing her to make a mess of it. But you ask whether there are other factors which evoke this criticism – I don't know. As I've said before, I really think it all stems from the fact that she's a woman.'

Brian Walden contended that Margaret Thatcher's strong political convictions led to some of the malicious abuse, that the Labour Party was politically much more violently opposed to her than it had been to previous Conservative leaders such as Harold MacMillan, Alec Douglas Home and Ted Heath: 'All in all, she frightens the Left, the Left Wing in general, certainly the Marxist Left because no Tory Leader in my time has been more straightforward in their condemnation of Marxism.' Did Lord George who is constantly warning of the dangers of left wing activists agree with Brian Walden's analysis?

'While agreeing with the general sentiment, I wouldn't explain it that way. You see, I don't think the Left of the Labour Party is Marxist.'He hesitated, then added, 'Some of them may well be. The Left of the Labour Party is a funny business at the moment; indeed, the Left in the country is a very peculiar business. I don't know whether I agree that there is a greater degree of opposition to her among the Labour Party than there was to, say, Mac-Millan. I well remember during the MacMillan era that right across the Party, including people like myself, there was an antipathy to MacMillan and what he seemed to stand for which certainly embraced a much wider spectrum of the Party than the current opposition to Mrs Thatcher. Consequently I don't really accept his premise. She certainly upsets the Left and she upsets quite a lot of other people in the Labour Opposition at the House of Commons because she is so bloody patently too good for their liking at dealing with them!' A wry smile of approval crossed his face.

In an article in the *Sunday Express* Lord George stressed Britain's urgent need for inspired and inspiring leadership. Had Margaret Thatcher's initial period in office given him grounds for optimism or was the optimism mingled with a hint of disappointment?

'It's not for me to be either satisfied or dissatisfied with her leadership – I'm not a Tory. I left the Labour Party for reasons which were made very clear at the time and which I've made very clear since, but I'm still a Social Democrat. I'm still on the Left. Therefore I wouldn't choose any Tory Leader – that's none of my business. Accordingly, the question of being disappointed in her doesn't arise. I only wish the bloody Labour Party were in a better state of health and organisation so that the question of having a Conservative Government didn't occur. But if you ask me do I think she has performed well, I think she herself as Prime Minister has performed a damn sight better than many of the team around her. I think she might have performed even better still if she had been able to fulfil her desire to deal with the wet, windy and woolly in her cabinet and had been able to dragoon that team into being stronger about a number of issues.'

As the title of Lord George's book *In My Way* suggests, he is well versed in the art of parliamentary warfare. He knows from personal experience of the realities and implications of standing alone, or almost alone, on certain specific issues. As a former Deputy Leader, he is fully aware of the difficulties a Prime Minister may encounter if the majority view in his Cabinet does not coincide with his own. If such a situation obtains, can the PM impose his will or are the difficulties almost insurmountable?

'It depends upon something which I really wouldn't know the answer to. A Prime Minister can always have his way if he has with him those people in the Cabinet who really matter in Party terms, or if his own standing both in the country and in the Party is sufficiently strong. If those circumstances prevail he can then afford to deal with the others. Now I don't know enough about the Conservative Party to know whether Mrs Thatchers' position in the Party or in the country is strong enough, and I haven't sufficient knowledge of the workings of the Cabinet to know whether she has enough of the strong men in the Cabinet siding with her. My guess, looking in from the

155

outside, is that the answer to both those questions is "no". That's my guess but I'm not a Tory so I don't know.

'So far as the Labour Party is concerned, Jim Callaghan wasn't able to carry his Cabinet with him; he is unable to carry his Shadow Cabinet with him now and I certainly take the view that Jim should move on. Wilson and I as a team - Leader and Deputy – always had trouble, always had difficulty because not only were we two very different people but we had different outlooks. On the other hand, Gaitskell and I never had any difficulty – and I was Deputy to both of them. Consequently a great deal does depend upon the immediate relations with other strong people in the Party. Now I had a power base of my own, as it were, in the Party which had to be taken into account; therefore, I'm sure Wilson would say if asked that he found me rather a handful and that I did inhibit some of the things he could do, at least I hope I did – we had enough trouble with the rest!' With a satisfied grunt and wry grin, he peered at me once again over the top of his glasses and continued, 'Therefore the same thing applies to Margaret.'

Lord Home commented, 'if a PM can't do certain things because of the views of the Cabinet, then it's probable that the PM's views ought to be modified, so you accept that – but it doesn't really arise?'

Lord George shrugged his shoulders. 'I don't know. . . I think if a Prime Minister *consistently* can't get things done pretty well the way he or she thinks they ought to be done, then there does come a time when you either have to change the team or the team has to change the Prime Minister – one or the other.' This observation seemed to amuse him and he paused for a momentary chuckle.

'Going back to the case of Wilson and myself,' he resumed, 'we managed it in a more or less civilised way over those seven years largely because we both wanted our strategy to work, but secondly because on several occasions I gave way when perhaps I shouldn't have done. But it is an impossible situation and I don't know what Alec Home meant by his observation, nor am I aware of the context of his remark. However, it doesn't at all follow that the

156

PM's views ought to be reduced or modified because the other blokes in the team don't agree. It is just worth the Prime Minister going back and thinking again, but if it went on like that for very long and over too many issues, well then something would have to give – in the case of Alec Home it did, and it did with Heath too.'

Ever since Margaret Thatcher has been in the forefront of British politics her opponents have claimed she is Right Wing. 'If Mrs Thatcher becomes Prime Minister,' they cried 'we will be living under the most Right Wing government this country has seen.' Lord George is a Social Democrat, to use his own words 'on the Left of British politics'; did he feel that Margaret Thatcher was on the Right?

'I don't think she is, you know, except in certain respects. One has to remember that Margaret Thatcher has certain limitations – there are only certain fields in which she has much experience. I'm told she's a very, very, able lawyer, in particular she's a tax lawyer, therefore one must assume a very great deal of expertise in that area, which is why I think she is so tough and strong about her chosen monetarist policies. She is a highly qualified chemist and therefore she knows a good deal about that technological side of life. I don't think she knows very much about industry. She knows comparatively little about foreign affairs, she's learning fast, but until she became Prime minister she wasn't qualified in that sphere; consequently, she doesn't really know much about that side of life. It seems to me there are gaps about Margaret Thatcher. There are some areas she knows superbly well and she clearly is very highly qualified in them. There are other areas in which she is less well qualified and that may be part of her problem at the moment. However, it doesn't detract from my overall regard for her as the Leader of her Party, or as the Prime Minister, or as a person; but if you're trying to give a balanced judgment of her, you must put forward both sides of the case.'

Some members of Parliament, notably Lord Home, have contended that civil servants are advisors rather than decision-makers. Nevertheless, several leading commentators embracing the whole spectrum of politics have taken the opposite view. It's difficult to imagine a forceful personality like Lord George succumbing to the will of the Civil Service, but to what extent does the Civil Service influence or thwart the decisions of Cabinet Ministers, Deputy Prime Ministers and even Prime Ministers?

'As much as you will let them. If you're at the top, know your job, are prepared to listen to advice, make your own mind up – and make your own mind up very clearly and explain it very clearly – you will always have your way, not theirs. That's very true of the Civil Service. But if you're a waffler, if you can't make your mind up, if you can't take decisions, if you are indecisive, then the Civil Service will take over.

'There's no *special* problem in the Civil Service, but there can be a problem. On the whole, the fellows who are at the top of the major departments – and I've served in seven in various capacities – are very qualified people, very able chaps. That's how they get there, at least for the most part – you occasionally get a weak one but obviously they know the job. The average Minister of Transport in this country has lasted for about nine months, or some bloody silly time like that. Ministers change very frequently. Civil servants tend to remain in their department for a long time so they know the ropes and therefore the Minister is at a certain disadvantage. Now that disadvantage can be overcome if you're a bit like me, it can't be overcome if you show any sign of weakness. I think it all depends on the person, but I would guess that Margaret has her way when she wants to have it,' pronounced Lord George with an amused smile.

It is widely acknowledged that the benefits accruing from the practice of monetarism take a long time to work through the economy. Several Ministers have publicly voiced their concern about the years of austerity that may lie ahead. The PM has talked about a long-term policy for the future and warned the nation that 'some things are going to get worse before they get better'. If the Government's policies

158

do not yield the anticipated rewards and benefits within the five-year term and the electorate become impatient and vote the Conservatives out of office, how do you see the future of this country given the present constitution of the Labour Party?

'Jesus! I will tell you a story that came up the other morning when I was talking to my wife. Now my wife is a Jew, one of my grandfathers was an Irishman and I read the other day in a newspaper that somebody had just discovered under the Irish Nationality Act of 1956 that anybody who had a grandparent born in Ireland is automatically an Irish citizen. I looked at my wife and said, "My dear, should this very thing you're talking about happen – should the Tories be voted out of office and the Labour Party in its present state be returned to power – we've got two choices: the Israelies will accept us because you are an Israeli citizen by their law, the Irish will accept us because apparently I'm an Irish citizen by their law – Darling, we've got two ways out!" In the present state of British politics, if such a situation occurred, it would worry me very much indeed. The whole tragedy is that there is no semblance of an alternative Government available given the present state of the Labour Party. I would hope that the Labour Party would re-establish itself fairly soon, but we're not discussing the Labour Party.'

Even the most ardent optimist would find it impossible to deny that Britain faces grave economic problems. Our industrial decline has been gathering force over a number of years and the continuing gloomy forecasts have perhaps cast a giant shadow on the initiative, drive, ingenuity and industry of the British people. It is widely accepted that we are on the brink of a world recession and that the threat to world peace has been augmented by the invasion of Afghanistan and the mounting tensions in the Middle East. In this precipitous climate any world leader has a daunting task. What qualities and strengths does Margaret Thatcher bring to the premiership?

'Well, she obviously can lead – she goes in front, which is a great change from some of the other buggers! She can

159

set a policy out. She can stick to it. She has decisiveness. She may get the wrong policies, but we're not arguing about the merits of the case. However, when she gets the policies and she gets her teeth into something she obviously can stick at it. Equally, we've seen some quite outstanding examples of where she's had the courage to swap horses in midstream, or whatever the simile may be. To take one specific example, she switched at Lusaka over Rhodesia. I didn't agree with the switch at the time, but looking back on it, it would be difficult to fault it now, and she certainly had the courage to do it.

'She has had the courage to backtrack on a number of issues – whether it was right or wrong to backtrack is not under examination here, but that takes a good deal of courage, particularly if you know, as she must know, that she's under this bloody constant surveillance. So she's got courage, she's got decisiveness and she has this ability to think things out. Whether she has too little emotion, whether she understands too little the impact on other people, I don't know – maybe she has that too. But whatever the answer to that question might be I regard her as outstandingly – not only as Butler once said of MacMillan, "the best Prime Minister we've got" – I think she's outstandingly the best Conservative Prime Minister available. And looking at the mess the Opposition are in, maybe she's the best Prime Minister available!'

A great deal of attention was focused upon the 1975 leadership contest. The outcome came as a surprise to most professional observers and at least for a while led to the formation of certain factious elements within the Conservative Party. Having witnessed the stewardship of both Leaders, what comparisons would you draw between the leadership of Margaret Thatcher and that of her predecessor?

'Oh well, she's incomparably better. I think she's an incomparably better person than Ted Heath. . . . Oh yes! I wouldn't be in favour of putting Heath back in her place! She's an incomparably better equipped person. What stubborness and obstinacy she has is better founded. He was

Above: Mrs Thatcher's Cabinet in the Pillared Room at No 10
Downing Street; below: at the Palace of Westminster for the State
opening of Parliament, which heralded Mrs Thatcher's new
Government

With former Prime Ministers James Callaghan, Harold Wilson and
Edward Heath following the unveiling of the Clement Attlee
memorial statue in the Members' Lobby of the House of Commons

a stubborn man full stop. However, as I say, I'm not in the Conservative Party, so it's not my business who they choose as their Leader, but as a Briton, as a subject of this country, I certainly think she is streets ahead of him.'

'We haven't the time to take our time' – how true that is of Britain today. The task of reversing our industrial decline is both enormous and immediate. As Margaret Thatcher commented, 'There aren't any easy options left for Britain.' The revenues from North Sea oil are not inexhaustible – time really is of the essence. In these particular circumstances, is there anyone else on the political scene you would prefer to see in the role of premier?

'At this moment, the straight answer to that is no there isn't. I repeat I'm still a Social Democrat so I'm not pretending to be a Conservative, but if you ask me is there anybody else I would rather see in that bloody seat at the moment given the present wretched state of British politics, the answer is a straight NO!'

Sir Geoffrey Howe – 'She expects you, if you hold different views very strongly, to argue your corner.'

The Chancellor of The Exchequer, The Right Honourable Sir Geoffrey Howe, QC, or Richard Edward Geoffrey, to give him his full name, is like many members of the House of Commons, a barrister by profession. A member of the Middle Temple, he was called to the Bar in 1952 and took silk in 1965. In the interim period he had on two occasions stood unsuccessfully as the Conservative Candidate for the constituency of Aberavon. He eventually entered Parliament in 1964 as the member for Bebington and now represents the constituency of East Surrey.

The grandson of a Welsh tinplate worker and son of a lawyer, Sir Geoffrey has possibly the most envied speaking voice in the Palace of Westminster, but at the drop of a hat he can lapse into an authentic South Wales dialect which both surprises and delights people who had hitherto been unaware of these imitative talents. Both he and Lady Howe were most courteous and charming hosts when I visited them at No. 11.

'I knew Margaret as a more or less contemporary from Oxford Conservatism,'Sir Geoffrey began, 'when I was at Cambridge I remember reading an article written by her in a publication called *The Oxford Tory* and wondered who this Margaret Roberts was – that was the first knowledge I had of her. I can't remember exactly how long after that it was when I first met her. Although we both practised at the Bar, I didn't do tax law so our paths didn't cross. The Tax Bar is a very select and exclusive section of the profession; I was at the Common Law Bar, at the more mundane end of things.

'When she became Secretary of State for Education, I was Solicitor General and we saw quite a lot of each other at that stage because I had to advise on the legal aspects of education law and the attitude the Government should take on the law relating to obscene literature and children. Then in 1972 I joined Ted Heath's Cabinet and it was during that period when we really came to know each other well. I found her very friendly and very informal, but she holds her views very strongly and she expects you, if you hold different views very strongly, to argue your corner. I think one of the things that surprises less direct temperaments is to find the explicit way in which she asserts her position, often at the beginning of a meeting, whereas I think civil servants as a breed, and men more than women as a sex, are more disposed to keep their cards close to their chest, not revealing their position until they are obliged to. It enables them to seem more judicial and to appear detached and objective. Of course, they're harbouring their own views just as clearly in their bosoms as anyone who openly declares them. I think it is that aspect of her personality

162

which is one of the unusual features about her. She very seldom leaves you in any doubt about what she is thinking and that invites you to be equally clear in response. I think you have to be very certain, and when you are with her assert your own point of view for fear of it not being heard, but then she is not alone in that.'

The Prime Minister and Sir Geoffrey Howe are inexorably pledged to pursue monetarist policies with ruthless determination, howl the Labour Party and Trade Union hierarchy. Had Sir Geoffrey always been an exponent of the practice and philosophy of monetarism, or had the failed economic policies of the past persuaded him to follow the teachings of Professor Friedman and tread the monetarist path?

'I don't want to be provoked into a lecture on monetarism, but monetarism is not a religion like Methodism or Calvinism; it's an aspect of economic truth which I think was disregarded. In my view, throughout the 1950s and 1960s the importance of monetary policy was neglected and it looked as though we as politicians could get along without it, but I don't think that either of us would claim to have been monetarists from the beginning of time – I certainly wouldn't. We were both members of the 1970–74 Government, which didn't take monetary policy as seriously as we do now, but then nor did anybody else. However, I do think some of us were becoming aware of this aspect of economic policy as that Government moved on towards its close, and Margaret was certainly one of those. I was less perceptive, I think, although I was actually an economic minister and she wasn't. But it depended very much at that stage on the views you were hearing from outside Government, the people you were talking to, the people you were listening to – I think we were all learning at different paces.'

And Professor Friedman?

'Oh yes, I admire him enormously!'

The Tory Party has been accused of being heartless. Government cuts have seemingly necessitated the closure of hospitals, centres for the disabled and old people's homes.

163

This is a particularly emotive issue and your opponents have exploited these emotions to the full. How would you answer your critics?

'At a whole host of different levels. I have always found it difficult to believe that anybody can sincerely and truthfully say that anyone who is involved in politics in a civilised democracy like Britain, can actually be involved in so heartless a fashion. Why do most people move into political activity? Because they care about the society they live in and one of the aspects of that society are the services available for those in greatest need. I would always, I think, do my opponents the credit of believing they were there because they cared.

Take it at a more cynical level: if you want to be elected in a democracy it would be foolish not to care about these things, not to appear to care about these things. The reality is that we are there because we believe we have the best policies for making society more prosperous, and if you make it more prosperous you are better able to care for people in the greatest need. All our policies are directed towards that aim.

'I was born and brought up in South Wales,' he said emotionally, 'and I fought two elections in 1955, and 1959 in my home town, where it was widely believed the Tories had horns and cloven hooves and the whole of my efforts were devoted to proving that was not so.'

Several leading economists have claimed that the cuts in public spending didn't go nearly far enough, that you merely held public expenditure at 1979 levels, instead of increasing it by the 3.5 billion intended by Labour. They further claim that if you had cut it in real terms it wouldn't then have been necessary to raise interest rates to their present high levels.

'Only the economists who agree with our strategy have put forward this argument and feel that we didn't go far enough; economists on the Left believe we were undertaking a foolish exercise in cutting public expenditure at all. In fact, if you look at what we have actually achieved and now plan to do, we are the first Government since the war to have produced spending plans which will be reducing public expenditure in real terms each year for the next four years. We shall be reducing it by about 1 per cent per year down by 4 per cent by 1983/4. We shall then be spending £11 billion less than Labour had planned. Now those are real reductions that will make a real difference.'

The oft-quoted propaganda views of the Labour Party is that the Tories are the party of the rich and that your Government in its first budget made the rich richer and the poor poorer. They claim that your policies are socially divisive, that far from uniting society they divide it and create two nations.

'It's a familiar line, but we were elected at the last election with support from a majority of working people in this country because on the track record since 1945 the Tory years have been years of greater prosperity than the years of the Labour Party. We believe that if you have a society which concentrates on making the rich poorer you end up by making the poor poorer as well. If you have a society which enables those with ability to become richer by their own efforts and to keep some of the rewards, if it's a society with a bit of zip about it, it's likely to have more prosperity so that the poor become richer too. You can't have a rich society unless you're prepared to have rich people! I don't think 'rich' is a nasty four-letter word. I think most people would like to have a rich society and I think they are prepared to see some people who are very rich if, as a consequence, the poor become richer, which is what we want to see.

'In my first budget, I gave income tax cuts to everybody. In fact the proportional tax cuts were bigger for the 'rich' because we have been losing a tremendous proportion of our most able people. Engineers, scientists, teachers, doctors, pop stars and actors were leaving these shores as a result of the absurdly high taxes they had to pay in this country. Now at least you are certain that you will keep 40 pence of the most prosperous pound you earn and people are coming back to this country; they are staying here, they are not emigrating, and people whose talents we very badly

165

need. Such a strategy makes total sense because it will help to make our society richer and the poor will become richer as well.

'It's important to remember that before the election Labour admitted they would have been obliged to raise taxes and reduce public spending. In my view they would have been raising taxes very substantially and offering no hope at all that we were going to see a change of direction. They would have been presiding over an increasing lack of economic success and inclining us, year by year, more and more in the direction of the least exhilarating of the Iron Curtain countries.'

The West's leading female politician has been portrayed in many and various ways since her election to the leadership of the Conservative Party and her arrival at 10 Downing Street. 'Iron Lady', a title which emanated from Moscow, is one of the earliest and perhaps the most famous description, while in France she is known as 'Madame Non'. West German Chancellor Helmut Schmidt is reputed, in a moment of pique, to have likened her to a rhinoceros. On the home front, Shadow Chancellor, Denis Healey, commented, 'She has an impenetrably thick hide, she is liable to mount charges in all directions and she is always thinking on the trot.' According to some members of the Press, Margaret Thatcher has a reputation for being impatient and talking through people. Is that a fair appraisal of her technique?

'No, it certainly isn't a fair appraisal.' Sir Geoffrey began to laugh, 'I can't, however, resist the temptation of saying that Denis Healey's alleged description of Margaret Thatcher amounts to a pretty good autobiographical description of himself! But I think they are all caricatures of caricatures of descriptions of Margaret. If by "Iron Lady" one means that she is a lady who manifestly has a very strong sense of purpose, then that's a fair description. I have already said that she believes in asserting her point of view, but she certainly doesn't talk through you. Discussion with Margaret has to be candid and firm but you are not dealing with a mind that conceals deep attitudes

166

which you are not able to test in discussion. You can test them. She expects you to.'

It has also been alleged in certain sections of the Press that the PM can be rude in argument.

'Oh she can be very forceful in argument. If justified, so can we all. But to quote the Press again, there was an instance recently when a senior civil servant was supposed to have said to the Prime Minister, 'That's absolute rubbish, if I may say so Prime Minister.' Now is that rude or not? I don't think it is. I think you are entitled to say that someone is talking nonsense. If Margaret Thatcher thinks you are wrong, if she thinks you are talking nonsense, she won't hesitate to tell you. But equally, were the roles to be reversed, she would expect to evoke a similar reaction; she would expect you to tell her she was talking nonsense. That is not rude. If by rude you mean discourteous, ill-mannered, churlish, no, she is not that.'

It has been rumoured that while Margaret Thatcher has become skilful in avoiding public confrontations, her basic difficulty lies in the fact that on many key issues she doesn't have a natural majority in her cabinet who share her deep-felt convictions and commitments. The media in general has focused upon the factious and continuing divisions between the 'hawks' and the 'doves' or the 'wets' and the 'non-wets'.

'I have never actually subscribed to the view that you can or should divide the Cabinet into groups of people who are committed to this or that decision or devoted to this or that cause. In my experience, everyone in the Cabinet is endeavouring to get the right answer; they are all trying to attain the same objectives, they all share the same basic commitments to Conservative policies, but there are bound to be differences of view as to the speed at which, the pace at which and the manner in which we make progress, and I don't think that Margaret would be as good a Prime Minister as she is unless she was at ease in that group of people. Now you are not at ease in a group of people if you feel day in and day out that you've got a little group of chaps who agree with you while the rest of them are diametrically opposed to you. She feels at ease with them because she knows we are all on the same side striving for the same objectives.

'The Press, who have a job to do, find it difficult to visualise any activity except in terms of a home win, away win or a draw; or, more dramatically, a victory, a defeat or a deadlock. Politicians try to avoid deadlocks. The business of politics is trying to find the way through that represents the right answer which is acceptable to the people you are trying to lead and work with. Consequently, the Cabinet would have to be a pretty rough and unusual place if it constantly consisted of people lining up on opposite ends of the room playing football against each other!'

'Punch-up Thursdays' is a phrase which has been frequently employed to describe these regular Cabinet meetings. Are they a reality or simply a fantasy of the media?

'Oh, of course there are *arguments*. There are some questions we have to solve which are difficult, which involve real differences of opinion where people argue very strongly about what is right and what is wrong, but I think there are very few occasions when people go away at the end of a discussion in Cabinet feeling that it hasn't been carried through to a proper conclusion. Although some members may well have adopted a different approach or come to a different conclusion, the answer can be regarded as the proper outcome of a proper discussion.'

Based on the hypothesis that the Prime Minister is deeply committed to implementing a particular policy, yet finds herself a lone voice in the Cabinet, can she enforce her view despite strong opposition, or would such a situation be both untenable and unrealistic?

'I think that Margaret Thatcher – any Prime Minister for that matter – can alter the character and nature of a Cabinet decision pretty decisively. As the Prime Minister is *primus inter pares*, she is entitled to give a lead, but to believe that the Prime Minister or anyone in the Cabinet would rush off on a jag of their own with which the whole of the Cabinet was out of sympathy is not realistic. It does

168

not work like that. But she can give a firmness, a decisiveness and a flavour to decisions which are her own.

If you take the whole discussion on the Community budget and the ensuing protracted negotiations, I can well imagine that if any other member of the Cabinet had been Prime Minister at this particular time they would have conducted those negotiations differently and I don't think that at the end of the day they would have made as much progress as she has. That's what leadership is all about. You have to be a very strong, forceful personality in order to get the job at all, but Margaret has an element in her make-up, a bone in her political body as it were, which does give her a quality of strength which is pretty remarkable!'

According to Rudyard Kipling 'the female of the species is more deadly than the male'. Margaret Thatcher appears to evoke venomous antagonism from her opponents; her policies are pure anathema to the Left, but is she more 'deadly' than previous Conservative Prime Ministers?

'One of the techniques of the Left in British politics is to denounce the present incumbent Conservative Leader or Prime Minister as a uniquely, grotesquely, obstinate, Right-Wing, neo-Fascist beast as it were, and to transform the immediate predecessor into an angel of sweetness, light and reasonableness. This is the kind of caricature process which has taken place recently. Margaret arrives, she leads the Tory Party to victory, and the Left-Wing Press immediately begin conjuring up names such as Attila the Hen, while lapel buttons appear showing her looking like some savage bird from outer space and she is caricatured as a uniquely savage Right-Wing monster.

'Meanwhile, Ted Heath is represented as angelic tranquility, as though people will forget that only five years ago it was *he* who was the obstinate, wilful, Right-Wing, doctrinaire Tory beast in contrast to the tranquil, benign wisdom of Alec Douglas Home who preceded him. Yet go back five years earlier and Alec Douglas Home was the wild Right-Wing anti-Communist who believed in nuclear weapons, did his economics in matchsticks and was a man

169

of un-wisdom compared with the benevolent tranquil, wise, almost Socialist Harold MacMillan who preceded him. Go back another five years and Harold MacMillan was the current devil, so in the light of the persistent comment of the Left media commentators you must always aim off for wind in assessing the characters of Conservative Leaders.'

Brian Walden observed that Margaret Thatcher had no desire to dissemble, a characteristic he found almost unique in the world of politics. He commented upon her continual willingness to express herself in an open, forthright manner without any attempt at circumlocution or concealment. 'This woman means what she says. That's what makes her the most exciting figure in British politics.'

'Oh yes, she is *dramatically* exciting! She has an openness, a frankness, an enthusiasm and an unwillingness to be cowed and overcome by tiredness which makes her enormous fun to work with. You can never be quite sure on issues you have never discussed with her what her instinctive reaction will be, but it's bound to be interesting. She is as willing as any politician to be pre-occupied with the difficulties of the situation. Britain has not been winning for many years and the business of turning us round so that we begin to become winners again instead of losers is very difficult and there are many days when you go into the office and yet again the cards seem to fall in the wrong way. In politics, as in any other walk of life, you just wonder when your lucky breaks are going to come back again. Now Margaret is quite undaunted by that. She is willing to be pre-occupied with the difficulties and discuss them because they have to be discussed, but you never feel that she is being overborne by them and she is able to show that even on the days when it isn't fun, she thinks it's well worth while having a try!'

Does she become very tense in times of stress and moments of crucial importance?

'Oh yes, I think at moments of importance, sometimes at particular moments of decision, sometimes when facing especially important debates or speeches, she becomes tense. But then I remember one of the things that was said to me very early on in my practice at the Bar by a senior silk who went on to become an Appeal Court Judge – unless you feel tense and nervous when you're about to do anything important, you're not going to do it well; apparently he never got up in court even to ask for a simple adjournment without having a slight sense of butterflies in the stomach. It's a very important observation. Tension is a necessary aspect of perfected performance.'

In an election speech in Manchester in 1906, Winston Churchill remarked, 'Men will forgive a man anything except bad prose.' How forgiving is the 'Iron Lady'?

Afer a long pause Sir Geoffrey replied: 'She would not lightly forgive disloyalty. She would forgive error and misjudgment, particularly if you were candid in discussing it with her. I think the only thing which would lead to her being less than forgiving of an error or misjudgment is if she thought your errors had become chronic, as she has little respect for a weathervane approach to issues. Accordingly, if you said to her, "Look, at one time I thought this, but now for the following reasons I think that and I was wrong in my earlier view," fine – she finds that perfectly understandable. But if you said "Five years ago I thought this, three years ago I thought that, one year ago I thought this and today I think that," then she doesn't find that easy to comprehend, because she is a politician of commitment for whom most views are very firmly and consistently held.'

It has been suggested that in her role as Leader of the Opposition Margaret Thatcher dispenses with many of the intricasies of conventionalism. She is a spontaneous, instinctive politician, who I suspect frequently surprises the more orthodox temperaments within Westminster. For example, her detailed account of the Anthony Blunt revelation astonished many MPs who had become accustomed to ambiguous statements on such delicate matters.

'Margaret *is* very different. The whole style of her approach to discussions with ministerial colleagues and civil servants is far less easily confined within the conventions. To take a curious example, most people perhaps don't realise that in Conservative Governments – I think

171

it's probably true of all Governments – at meetings of Cabinet committees as well as in Cabinet, people are addressed by their title. You do not say "Keith said this, Jim said that and Willie said the other thing". You say "the Industry Secretary said this", "the Employment Secretary mentioned that" and "I must say I disagree with the Home Secretary". It has a value in the sense that it reminds people of the importance of decisions they are taking. That was very firmly maintained in my experience in the last Conservative Government by all members. It's very unusual to have people lapsing into conversational style over the ministerial committee table. Now Margaret is much more likely, quite spontaneously, to say "But Peter wants that", "Jim wants this", or "Surely that can't be right, can it, Geoffrey?", then the conventions re-establish themselves. But I think it's an impatience with conventions that involve a waste of time and which don't seem to be entirely necessary which gives rise to this approach. I find it difficult to know whether that convention is right or wrong, but Margaret is certainly more inclined to be informal.'

According to rumbles emanating from Whitehall, the PM has created a precedent by her frequent visitations to various departments, formerly the hallowed ground of the Civil Service. More than one civil servant has been heard to remark, somewhat apprehensively, that she arouses a feeling of trepidation among the more timorous souls.

'I don't know whether other Prime Ministers have carried out this practice, but undoubtedly Margaret has been visiting various departments. While I have not seen her on those occasions I have frequently seen her in consultation with senior civil servants and again I think there is a touch of the unconventional because there is a degree of openness about her approach.

'My impression is that civil servants find it very refreshing to have someone with clear views who is giving clear leadership to a country which God knows sadly needs it! They, too, have adjusted to the fact that if they feel the PM is about to embark upon a course or indeed express

172

a view they think is wrong, then they are there to say so. If a case is worth making and it can be argued properly, then it is a case that Margaret Thatcher will listen to. However, it must be a new experience for civil servants, as well as it is for some politicians, to be required to argue forthrightly on the realities of an issue rather than debating round the edges.'

A senior minister is reputed to have remarked, 'Her initial instincts are almost invariably wrong.' Conversely, Brian Walden contended, 'Margaret's instincts are her own best guide,' while another bemused critic lamented despairingly, 'But she conforms to no previous rules.' As someone once said, 'Those who have done most for the world have been the dissenters and the non-conformists.'

'Well, I think in terms of style and character it's because she's different that she is where she is now, and it is that which gives one a sense of hope. I think it's an oversimplification to say her instincts are always right or her instincts are invariably wrong. One of her great virtues is that she is prepared to acknowledge and respond to instinctive views so that she's reacting like a human being. Margaret reacts in an instinctive way. She is very natural, she's spontaneous, she says "That's right" or "That's wrong"! I would certainly think her instinct is more often right than wrong, but sometimes it can be wrong. This is the importance of being able to debate things with her. If her initial response is one which people want to question, she is prepared to consider opposite views, but she has strong instincts and she responds instinctively.'

President Machel, the Marxist President of Mozambique, observed that Margaret Thatcher was the best Prime Minister for fifteen years because she had the courage to solve the Rhodesian problem.

'In my view the most interesting factor is the extent to which people outside as well as inside this country do recognise that in Margaret's arrival at No 10 a powerful force has been added to the political scene during the last quarter of the twentieth century. Something really new has happened and arrived. Not unique – there have been other national leaders around the world since the end of the war who have added a dimension to the international political scene, but Margaret certainly numbers among them. That in itself helps to raise the self confidence of our country. When she is criticised for being obstinate, tiresome and tenacious at summit meetings, for obstinate, tiresome and tenacious read determined, committed and courageous. This is a public recognition of the change of dimension she has brought about.'

During the past few years we appear as a nation to have become increasingly prone to expressing self doubts about our ability to transcend our domestic problems and to regain our prestige both in the universal marketplace and in the sphere of world influence. Somewhere along the road we seem to have lost our self-confidence. On countless occasions Margaret Thatcher has stated, 'I am doing what I passionately believe to be right for Britain and I'm going to keep on doing it.' She exudes confidence but can she enthuse it in others? Can she galvanise the nation?

'Given the extent to which Britain in recent years has been the victim of illusions, delusions and myths and the mistaken belief that we can always look to somebody else to get things right, we needed desperately at this time someone with the candour and the courage to tell people the truth, someone who would go on sticking to policies which are going to be difficult, someone with a sense of vision. Margaret pre-eminently fulfils that need.

'Above all, she gives me confidence because she will remain tenaciously committed to the course which is necessary for our nation to recover prosperity and self-confidence. That is very important. The knowledge that there is a tenacity and a courage which can somehow sparkle in a human way and convey its enthusiasm, the knowledge that we have Margaret at the helm at this particular time in our nation's history is enormously encouraging. We have a chance of winning!'

9

The Citadel

Having heard the views and opinions of some of Margaret Thatcher's most notable contemporaries, let us now look back at 1978 and the events that led up to the 1979 election. The year 1978 was memorable for the endless speculation concerning the possible date of the General Election. Prime Ministerial announcements were constantly scrutinized to see whether they contained a veiled hint as to the timing of this vitally important landmark. As springtime gave way to summer, September or October were favoured as the two most likely months for the staging of what would probably be the last election of the nineteen seventies.

Eventually it was announced from Downing Street that Prime Minister Callaghan was to broadcast on the evening of 7th September and while MPs from all parties waited with bated breath to hear the words which would fundamentally affect their lives in the days and months to come, the public looked forward to a definite end to all the speculation. But to the surprise of most of the political world and no doubt to the consternation of many of his own MPs, supporters and Trade Union leaders, Mr Callaghan informed the country that he had decided to 'go on'. He justified his decision by claiming that 'inflation is at its lowest level for some years; taxes were cut during the summer; increases in social benefits will take place this autumn; and living standards are generally improving.

'Now I have seen it said that I have rigged this temporary boom in order to win an election. That is false. The benefit the country is experiencing today is the result of your efforts, and the Government has eased the situation because we thought the economy could stand it, and for no other reason. These can be lasting, not temporary improvements if we follow consistent policies. . . .

'We can see the way ahead. With prices now more

stable, with steadier growth, with the increasing advantage brought by North Sea oil, with good foreign exchange reserves, we can foster industrial confidence, and we have already laid the foundations to create a better life for our people. I know we have large and positive support in the country for the way we are facing our problems. So when I met the cabinet this morning I invited ministers to prepare themselves for the fifth and final session of this Parliament. We shall work with greatest vigour to control inflation, to reduce unemployment and to improve the efficiency and prosperity of British industry. We shall face our difficulties as we come to them. I can already see some looming on the horizon. I cannot and don't promise that we shall succeed. I can say that we shall deserve to.

'But basically I want to say to you that we go on because we are doing what is best for Britain. Let's see it through together.'

Earlier that day Margaret Thatcher remarked that she didn't imagine Mr Callaghan would broadcast to say he wasn't calling an election, but after that event she admitted she had been misled. 'What's he going to have when there is an election?' she commented. 'People were expecting an election and they thought it was the right time to hold one. To frustrate that feeling is a mistake.' In a written statement to the Press she asserted that the Prime Minister's decision was against the nation's interest. 'He has lost his majority and with it the authority to govern. He should now properly seek the verdict of the people.

'There are indeed many problems to be settled in industry, commerce, jobs, the social services, Rhodesia, defence. They need long term solutions, not short-term expedients. They need a Government with a clear mandate from the people and several years' life. Only that would restore confidence. As it is, we shall now have a long period of election fever. The country belongs to the courageous, not to the timid.'

In a ministerial broadcast on the evening of 8th September, Margaret Thatcher amplified her statement and exercised her right of reply. In particular, she joined issue

176

with one of Mr Callaghan's main contentions:

'He said that he was afraid that if he held an election now, people might say that he had staged a pre-election boom. Boom? What boom? There have been more people out of work over the last year than at any time since the war. Since 1974 food prices have more than doubled, tax has more than doubled. This Labour Government has almost the worst record of any government in the developed world. Despite the advantages of North Sea oil, we're just about bottom of the league on any measure you care to take, and that's no place for Britain.

'Mr Callaghan also said that none of our problems this winter would be solved by an election now. Well some of us look further ahead than this winter. We don't believe that Britain has to grind on in bottom gear. The longer he puts things off, the worse they'll become, and the worse they become the longer it will take to put them right.

'But I believe they can be put right, once we've got a Government that has confidence. The confidence of the people and confidence in the people. A Government with authority at home, and with authority abroad. In a world full of danger what can a broken-backed Government do to defend Britain's interests, to strengthen the free world, to help end the bloodshed in Rhodesia?

'I think you've got the right to choose whether we should drift aimlessly on, or whether we should move in a new and positive direction. This time last year Mr Callaghan said "Back us or sack us". Well one day, and it can't be put off for ever, you'll have the chance to give your answer.'

The Party Conferences, which few people had expected to be featured in the 1978 political calendar, became a necessary focal point for the Party Leaders to rekindle the flames of enthusiasm among their party workers – workers who had been keyed up for an election since the beginning of 1978, or was it 1977, or 1976? For a moment it seemed almost impossible to recall a time when the nation wasn't put on a general alert for what Margaret Thatcher had described as a 'watershed election'. In her conference speech at Brighton which was the occasion of her 53rd birthday, she spoke these words:

'Our Party offers the nation nothing less than national revival, the deeply-needed, long-awaited and passionately longed-for recovery of our country. That recovery will depend on a decisive rejection of the Labour Party by the people and a renewed acceptance of our basic Conservative belief that the State is the servant, not the master of this nation.

'Let me now turn to something deeply damaging to this country. Many of us remember the Labour Party as it used to be. In the old days it was at least a party of ideals. You didn't have to agree with Labour to understand its appeal and respect its concern for the underdog. Gradually over the years there has been a change. I have no doubt those ideals, those principles, are still alive today in the hearts of traditional Labour supporters. But among those who lead the Labour movement something has gone seriously wrong.

'Today, instead of the voice of compassion, the croak of the Quango is heard in the land. There may not be enough jobs for the workers, but there are certainly plenty of jobs for the boys. Many in the Labour Party wonder what has happened to it. Socialism has gone sour. Today, Labour seems to stand too often for expediency, for greed, for privilege, for policies that set one half of society against the other. There are many reasons for this. One stems from the least attractive of emotions, envy. This spirit of envy is aimed not only at those privileged by birth and inherited wealth, like Mr Wedgwood Benn. It is also directed against those who have got on by ability and effort. It is seen in Labour's bias against men and women who seek to better themselves and their families. Ordinary people – small businessmen, the self-employed – are not to be allowed to rise on their own. They must rise collectively or not at all.

'Object to merit and distinctions, and you're setting your face against quality, independence, originality, genius, against all the richness and variety of life. A society like that cannot advance. Our civilisation has been built by generation after generation of men and women inspired by

178

the will to excel. Without them, we would still be living in the Stone Age. Without the strong, who would provide for the weak? When you hold back the successful you penalise those who need help.

'Envy is dangerous, destructive, divisive – and revealing. It exposes the falsity of Labour's great claim that they're the party of care and compassion. Envy is the worst possible emotion to inspire a political party supposedly dedicated to improving the lot of ordinary working people. From there it is but a short step to the doctrine of class warfare. The Marxists in the Labour Party preach that this is not only just, but necessary and inevitable.

'But let me put this thought to you: if it's wrong to preach race hatred – and it is – why is it right to preach class hatred? If it's a crime to incite the public against a man simply because of the colour of his skin – and it is – why is it virtuous to do so just because of his position?

'The political organization of hatred is wrong – always and everywhere. Class warfare is immoral, a poisonous relic of the past. Conservatives are as fallible, as human and therefore as given to making mistakes as the next man. But we do not preach hatred and we are not a party of envy.

'Those who claim we are a class party are standing the truth on its head. So, too, are those who claim we are racists. . . . It is true that Conservatives are going to cut the number of new immigrants coming into this country, and cut it substantially, because racial harmony is inseparable from control of the numbers coming in. But let me say a word to those who are permanently and legally settled here, who have made their homes with us. Your rights, your responsibilities, are the same as those of every other British citizen: and your opportunities ought to be.

'May I end on a personal note? Long ago, I learnt two lessons of political life: to have faith and to take nothing for granted. When we meet again the election will be over. I would not take the result for granted. But I have faith that our time is coming. I pray that when it comes we use it well; for the task of restoring the unity and good name

179

of our nation is immense.

'I look back at the great figures who led our Party in the past, and after more than three years I still feel a little astonished that it has fallen to me to stand in their place. Now, as the test draws near, I ask your help. And not only yours. I ask it of *all* men and women, who look to us today, who share with us our longing for a new beginning. Of course we in the Conservative Party want to win; but let us win for the right reason – not power for ourselves, but that this country of ours, which we love so much, will find dignity and greatness and peace again.

'Three years ago I said we must heal the wounds of a divided nation. I say it again today with even greater urgency. There is a cause that brings us all together and binds us all together. We must learn again to be one nation, or one day we shall be no nation. That is our Conservative faith; it is my personal faith and vision. As we move towards government and service, may it be our strength and inspiration. Then, not only will victory be ours, but we shall be worthy of it.'

The events of 1978 were consigned to memory and the pages of history and after the reassuring normality of the annual Christmas celebrations people looked forward to the year ahead with a mixture of hope and scepticism. But the new year, far from heralding a new beginning, ushered in a wave of industrial chaos which was described by the Press as the worse spate of strikes since 1926. The long-suffering British public reeled under the effects of hospital closures, school closures, lightning tube strikes and the cessation of services by graveyard diggers. But while they were assiduously picking their way through the rubbish, hoping to avoid a chance encounter with a local rodent, the Prime Minister arrived back from a summit meeting in sunny Guadaloupe. When pressed at the airport for a comment on Britain's crisis by a host of frenetic reporters, an irate Mr Callaghan uttered the immortal words 'Crisis, what crisis?' – a statement that will surely haunt him and taunt him for the rest of his life. He had made a serious and perhaps fatal misjudgment both of the political climate

and of the mood of the country. It was greeted by the
public with abject horror, almost incredulity – surely he
wasn't being serious; after all, he had only been out of the
country for a few days.

These proved to be disastrous months for the Labour
Government. The 'special relationship' they claimed with
the unions fell into total disarray. The icy blasts of '79
came to be known and always will be known as the winter
of their discontent.

As the dark, bleak winter days began to recede and make
way for the approach of spring, the rubbish continued to
pile up in the streets and reached mountainous heights.
Once again the wise fraternity of the media, pundits and
astrologers gazed into their crystal balls and tried to predict
the date on which the nation would determine its future.
For many years the electorate, while obviously anxious for
their own particular party to emerge as the victors,
appeared to have taken the view that in the last analysis
there really wasn't any fundamental difference between
the two major parties. It was frequently said that once the
victors were seated in the corridors of power at Westminster
the effect on everyday life would be minimal.

In the late seventies the climate changed dramatically.
Politicians and commentators alike saw a fundamental
difference between the two main parties. A difference of
approach and policy which was so fundamental and far-
reaching that it would determine the shape of society for
years to come, or perhaps, depending on the mood and
resolve of the British people, for ever.

Brian Walden, who contended that the most vital issue
in British politics was whether we really existed to serve
the State or whether the State existed to serve us, commented upon the leaders of the two major parties. 'I look
to Margaret Thatcher to change the relationship between
the citizen and the state. . . . I think she believes in all the
classic verities of English liberty, and so do I. I still think
they are absolutely valid and I would like to see them
tried. . . . She is a defender of a liberal society; she's not a
Social Democrat. She doesn't want the State to play an

181

ever-increasing role. She's the English person writ large – that's her greatest asset. She should not listen to all the siren voices like Jim Prior who want her to turn herself into a Callaghan in skirts. I'm always annoyed when she listens to people who want to change her. If they change her, they will lose her unique appeal . . . and she will lose.

'However, if you want someone who will carry you on down the present road, there's nothing much wrong with Mr Callaghan, who is no fanatic and no Marxist. He is a respectable Western Social Democratic politician, prepared to give way to the unions and prepared to give way to the world of the State, prepared to take us gently down that path. If that's what the British people want, they should vote for him. Her appeal is that she isn't like that.'

Nineteen-seventy-nine was the year of another vitally important landmark, repercussions of which were to have a significant effect upon the fortunes, or rather misfortunes, of the Labour Party. The setting up of separate assemblies for Scotland and Wales were two of the main pledges in the Labour Party manifesto. During protracted proceedings in the House of Commons, the Government suffered a number of defeats and was eventually forced into accepting a referendum on the issue. Additionally, as a result of a revolt by some of the Government's own back-benchers, Parliament decreed that 40 per cent of those entitled to vote had to vote 'yes', otherwise the Government was required to lay orders before Parliament for the repeal of the Scotland and Wales Act.

The date for the referendum was set for 1st March and MPs from all parties hurried and scurried round the countryside, on the one hand extolling the virtues of separate assemblies, on the other warning of the inherent dangers and likelihood of the break-up of the United Kingdom.

Polling day arrived, and the people of Scotland and Wales, or at least some of them, went to the booths to register their vote. On the morning of 3rd March the *Daily Telegraph* carried the headline 'Black Eye and a Half for Labour Devolution Plan'.

In Wales the rejection was unequivocal: 47 per cent of the electorate voted 'no' and only 12 per cent voted in favour. In Scotland, 36 per cent of those eligible to vote simply stayed at home and while 51 per cent of those who actually voted said 'yes', it fell far short of the requirement laid down by Parliament that 40 per cent of those entitled to vote should say 'aye'. Taking the figure as a whole, those in favour of devolution were 33 per cent and against 31 per cent.

While the results were undeniably damaging to the tottering minority Labour Government, they were greeted as something of a triumph by the Conservative Party who had campaigned for a 'no' vote in both Scotland and Wales. In the ensuing days the Prime Minister's dilemma was considerable, the atmosphere in the House of Commons electric and speculation about the forthcoming election rife. Could Jim fix it yet again?

The excitement mounted, and the corridors of power reverberated with gossip. Then the long-awaited announcement concerning the PM's intention on Devolution was made. On 22nd March a solemn Mr Callaghan broadcast to the nation. On the Scottish issue he pointed out that 'A majority of those who voted did, in fact, vote in favour of the proposal to set up a separate Assembly. But the majority in favour was not large enough to fulfil the conditions that Parliament had laid down beforehand. So the Referendum result, instead of ending the argument as we had hoped, has heightened it. In the light of the result, the Secretary of State for Scotland is required to lay before Parliament an order to repeal the Act in its entirety. But of course it isn't enough to lay such an order: Parliament must be able to debate it and to decide on it. The Government therefore believes there should be a short, intermediate stage between laying the order which the Secretary of State has done today and asking the House to vote on it.

'Now some are saying that they won't sit down and talk about these matters until the present Act has been wiped off the Statute Book. But surely that isn't very sensible. If the Act was repealed at this moment we should be left with a vacuum. The Act would have disappeared as a result of a Parliamentary vote, but we would have nothing to put in its place, despite the Referendum result. So before the Government asks Parliament to vote we have offered talks with all the other parties separately to endeavour to come to some agreement that would be for the benefit of Scotland and enhance the unity of the United Kingdom. . . .

'As for Wales, the position isn't the same. Unlike Scotland there is no strong pressure to retain the Act and I have no doubt that in due course Parliament will repeal it. One valuable result of the recent campaigns and the Referendum has been to kill stone dead any idea that those who advocate separating Wales or Scotland from the rest of Britain have a significant following. They haven't.'

The following evening Margaret Thatcher was given the opportunity to put her side of the Devolution question. She exercised her right of reply with an air of quiet confidence.

'During the long debates on devolution', said Mrs Thatcher, 'our overriding aim has been to preserve the unity of our country, that is to keep England, Scotland, Wales and Northern Ireland together. Many times, when the Government forced their legislation through Parliament, we called for all-party talks on this question. Always the Government turned us down. Even as recently as last month Mr Callaghan described our proposals as "a sham and a shower"; I think that was a mistake. It seems to me that he only wants talks when he's in difficulties, not when there's time for them to succeed.

'As the Bills for Scotland and Wales were debated in Parliament, so the doubts and anxieties about them grew. So last summer Parliament decided that the people of Scotland and Wales should have their say. As it happened, only one in eight people in Wales supported the Government's plans. In Scotland one in three. And if you consider that the reason why many didn't vote at all was because Government ministers said that not to vote was the same as voting 'No', it's clear there was a substantial opposition to the particular scheme of devolution that was on offer.

184

In our view, therefore, there is no basis for going ahead with the Act. Three weeks ago we had the results. By now Parliament should have been given the opportunity to take a final decision. Instead, the Government's trying to buy time.

'The devolution issue, and the way it's been handled, are the occasion for us to put down the 'No Confidence' motion. But they are far from being the whole reason. We're in a period of great uncertainty. The danger is that measures are considered, and steps taken with a view to their immediate affect, rather than to what will happen in the long term. Even if this Parliament were to run its full span, there are only about three working months left. Any discussions on devolution would inevitably be over-shadowed by thoughts of the coming election. I don't think that's the way to consider matters as important as the government of Scotland and Wales and indeed the whole United Kingdom. So the right way to proceed is to have that election now. Then we can treat these vital matters, and many others that are so important to us all with the consideration they merit, with a new Parliament, a fresh mandate from the people, a new Government and a long lease of life ahead. If as I hope the minority parties join with us next Wednesday, we shall not only be able to set the wheels in motion. We shall also have reasserted the historic right of the House of Commons to say to the Government of the day "enough is enough".'

Seemingly, Margaret Thatcher's broadcast created a favourable impression. David Harris of the *Daily Telegraph* was prompted to remark: 'After her reply was over, MPs must have been left wondering why on earth Mr Callaghan gave her the opportunity to fire what sounded almightily like the shots of an election campaign by himself making his ministerial broadcast on Thursday night. What he had achieved in his broadcast was difficult to see as it was completely eclipsed that evening by Mrs Thatcher's decision to put down her No Confidence motion.'

During the following six days the atmosphere was charged with anxiety, expectancy and excitement. There was a buzz of activity behind the scenes, a great deal of wheeling and dealing and much head counting. The media with its hourly news bulletins expended its maximum effort on trying to work the public up into a near frenzy about the likely outcome of the 'No Confidence' motion.

When dawn broke on the morning of March 28th, the air was clear and cold and the headline in *The Daily Telegraph* read simply 'Callaghan Scramble for Votes'.

Throughout the course of this vital day the outcome still remained uncertain. Rumours about the voting intentions of some members of the minor parties were widespread. Some said that Enoch Powell held the key to the Government's fate, others contended that Gerry Fitt or Frank Maguire held the balance, but no one could predict with any degree of certainty whether the Government would survive the day.

As the Prime Minister and Leader of the Opposition prepared themselves for the long and gruelling hours that lay ahead the tension mounted. By early afternoon the Chamber was packed to capacity, bulging at the seams with expectant faces. The Press, MPs wives, friends and diplomats were virtually hanging over the gallery, straining to catch a glimpse of the main participants in one of the most dramatic parliamentary occasions for half a century. When the leading lady, dressed in a black-and-white check suit, walked centre-stage just after 3 pm to move the motion of 'No confidence in Her Majesty's government' the atmosphere was electric.

The heroine, depending upon your political affiliations, delivered her oration for approximately half an hour, ending with these words:

'What condemns the Prime Minister is the justified feeling that the substance of matters before the House takes second place to the survival of the Government. That feeling is widespread and it robs this Government and the Prime Minister of authority, credibility and dignity. The only way to renew the authority of parliamentary government is to seek a fresh mandate from the people, and to seek it quickly. I challenge the Government to do so before

186

this day is through.'

It was now the turn of the leading man to take the stage. Dressed in a well-cut dark suit, and looking tall and confident, he proceeded to pour scorn on the leading lady's dialogue, claiming that she appeared to be under the misapprehension that her proposals were entirely new when in reality she was offering nothing more than the outdated policies of yesteryear.

The speeches over, each side frantically cheered their leader amidst a generous splashing of boos, yaboos, cries of rubbish and heeer heeeres. The two leading actors had played their part; now it was the turn of the supporting cast, who trouped on to the stage one by one and engaged in thrust and counter-thrust. Dusk fell, the evening drew in and Mr Michael Foot, Leader of the House, rose to make the closing speech. Then the moment that everyone had been waiting for finally arrived. It was 10 pm MPs rushed into the lobby to cast their votes. As they streamed back into the Chamber the tension was almost unbearable. No one knew which way the vote would go.

Margaret Thatcher sat rigidly on the Opposition Front Bench looking pale and tired. The tellers counted furiously, then suddenly the figure of James Hamilton, the Government teller on the Opposition lobby, appeared frantically waving a piece of paper announcing the total number of MPs who had voted for the 'No confidence' motion. He gave a thumbs-up sign to the Labour benches and Mr Callaghan beamed with satisfaction. His supporters let out a loud cheer and teased and taunted the glum looking Conservatives who sat opposite.

Mrs Thatcher looked tense and desolate, but within a few seconds the statuesque figure of Mr Spencer le Marchant was seen standing over her. He whispered something in her ear and a look of utter relief crossed her face; she relaxed her grip on the bench. At 22.18 hours it was announced that the Government of Mr James Callaghan had been defeated by just one vote, the Opposition Whip proclaiming that the Conservative motion of no confidence had been carried by 311 votes to 310.

187

The Tories erupted into loud, ecstatic cheers and their triumphant roar echoed through the Chamber. On the Government benches the ministers and their supporters sat stony-faced, momentarily stunned into shocked silence. It was an extraordinarily dramatic climax to one of the most exciting days the Commons had witnessed for many a year. Mr William Whitelaw, beaming benevolently, gently put his arm round Margaret Thatcher and the strain and tension of the past week ebbed away.

She had won! Mr Callaghan had become the first Prime Minister to be driven out of office and forced into a general election since the defeat of Ramsay Macdonald in 1924. Going straight to the Despatch Box he proclaimed with an air of dignified defiance, 'Mr Speaker, now that the House of Commons has declared itself, we shall take our case to the country. Having explained that he would ask the Queen to dissolve Parliament 'as soon as essential business can be cleared up', he continued, 'I will announce as soon as maybe – and that will be as soon as possible – the date of dissolution, the date of the election, and the date of the meeting of the new Parliament.'

With an air of equal dignified defiance, Mrs Thatcher, amidst frenzied Tory cheers, rose to her feet and stated: 'As the Government no longer has authority to carry on business without the agreement of the Opposition, I make it quite clear that we shall facilitate any business which requires the agreement of the Opposition, so that dissolution can take place at the very earliest opportunity and that the uncertainty be over.' While the Opposition benches continued with their celebrations, a group of Labour MPs found solace in the singing of The Red Flag.

Meanwhile, a weary but jubilant Mrs Thatcher, her head held high, returned to her home in Flood Street, where her husband Denis, overcome with pride, muttered 'Marvellous, marvellous' again and again. As Mrs Thatcher said, it had been an historic day – 'Exciting! A night like this comes once in a lifetime!'

Within seconds of the historic vote being taken, the battle

188

lines were well and truly drawn. It was widely predicted that the campaign would be one of the bitterest and fiercest in living memory. For the proposed date of the election Margaret Thatcher was believed to favour 26th April, but Labour wanted a longer campaign, culminating in an election in May.

Though she rejoiced in her hour of triumph, the Opposition Leader was fully aware of the supreme task which lay ahead; the real battle had only just begun. 'In politics,' she had said, 'you learn to take nothing for granted.' With her hopes high and her troups gathered around her, she hurled herself into combat with immense vigour and enthusiasm.

On the evening of 29th March, the Liberals scored a dramatic victory over Labour in the Edge Hill by-election and the Conservative Party, much to the dismay of its supporters, suffered the humiliation of losing their deposit. Seemingly undaunted, Margaret Thatcher visited her Finchley constituency the following day. She was all smiles as she shook hands with well-wishers. It was a happy day, filled with the dizzy anticipation of the events that lay ahead. But the joy and elation of bringing down the Government was to be cruelly and tragically shattered.

Just before 3 pm on Friday, 30th March, Airey Neave went to collect his car from the members' underground car park at the House of Commons. As Big Ben was about to strike the hour there was a loud explosion: Mr Neave was halfway along the exit ramp when the device went off in his car. A muffled rumble was heard in the House where a debate was in progress and Gerry Fitt, the Ulster MP, raised his arms in the air and murmured 'Bomb'. Meanwhile, one of Margaret Thatcher's aides, taking her to one side, informed her quietly that a bomb had exploded within the apparently secure precincts of the Mother of Parliaments and that someone had been killed. A look of total horror crossed her face. She appeared pale and shaken, but at that moment she had no idea who the victim was. She returned to the House immediately, where she was told that the murdered victim was her close friend and confidant

Airey Neave. She was stunned into shocked silence. Iron Lady she may be, courageous she undoubtedly is, but her grief was almost too much to bear. She once said she had been taught never to show her emotions in public but on that horrific day she couldn't disguise her grief nor hold back the tears. She rushed to Marsham Street, Westminster, where Airey had lived with his wife and later that evening she paid this moving tribute to her friend and hero, the man whose faith and inspiration had given her the incentive to stand for the leadership of the Conservative Party: 'The assassination of Airey Neave has left his friends and colleagues as stunned and grief-striken as his family. He was one of freedom's warriors. Courageous, staunch, true, he lived for his beliefs and now he has died for them. A gentle, brave and unassuming man, he was a loyal and very dear friend. He had a wonderful family who supported him in everything he did. Now, there is a gap in our lives which cannot be filled.'

The entire nation was saddened and shocked by the appalling tragedy, and tributes poured in from all over the country. Prime Minister James Callaghan said 'This abhorrent act has robbed our country of a distinguished public figure and a very brave man. No effort will be spared to bring his murderers to justice and to rid the United Kingdom of the scourge of terrorism.' Liberal Leader David Steel said, 'Airey Neave was one of the kindest and most respected members of the Commons. To my generation he was also a war hero because of his exploits at Colditz.' Northern Ireland MP Gerry Fitt said, 'Those responsible for his death may have killed a friend rather than an enemy.' He then recounted what Mr Neave had told him the previous night when they shared a taxi together: 'If the Tories win the election I will investigate the allegations of ill-treatment against suspected terrorists in Northern Ireland. If I find that any policemen have been interrogating people like that, they will feel the full brunt of my wrath. I know what it's like to be interrogated. I was interrogated by the worst – the Gestapo!'

Jim Prior, Shadow Employment spokesman, wept outside the House of Commons as he said, 'This is especially terrible for Mrs Thatcher. She and Mr Neave were very close.'

The man who had survived the horrors of the Gestapo, who had been the first man to escape from Colditz and who had risked his life on countless occasions so that others could escape to freedom had finally been murdered in the country he loved so much.

Airey Neave had the most distinguished war record in the House of Commons. Having escaped from Colditz he returned to England in May 1942 and masterminded an operation which organised the underground escape lines for the RAF. M 19, as it was known, secured the freedom of thousands of servicemen. In 1942 he was awarded the Military Cross, in 1945 he received the DSO and in 1947 the OBE. But his honours were not confined to his birthplace. The French awarded him the Croix de Guerre, the Americans the Bronze Star, Holland made him an Officer of the Order of Orange, and the Polish honoured him with the Order Polonia Restitua.

This, then, was Airey Neave, whose memory will live on in the hearts and minds of all those who cherish freedom and the dignity and rights of the individual.

In 1978, when I interviewed Airey Neave, he said of Margaret Thatcher: 'It required very considerable courage for a woman to stand for the leadership, particularly when it was rather unexpected and she will get to the top – she will be at No 10, of that I have no doubt.'

The date of the election had been announced: 3rd May 1979 was the day on which the nation would go to the polls to decide its fate for the future. Margaret Thatcher had to call upon all her reserves of courage and resilience to withstand the intensive pressures which crowded in upon her daily without the man who had stood so loyally by her side over the past years.

The campaign was, as anticipated, long, arduous and bitterly fought. 'Man is by nature a political animal,' said Aristotle, but while many would challenge his judgment, even those who normally take an essentially detached and cynical view of politics found it difficult not to be caught up in election fever – indeed there was little choice. As you switched on your radio in the early hours of the morning details of the latest opinion polls blared forth. Political commentators, sounding intense and with a deep sense of urgency, commented on their findings, while MPs were rushed into the studios to comment on the commentators.

At 10 am there were regular Press conferences. This was the occasion when the Party Leaders paraded their star generals to answer a whole host of questions from the eager men and women of Fleet Street. The Party Leaders, ministers and their aides, followed in hot pursuit by photographers and members of the media, spent their days and nights scampering round from one end of the country to the other. Some went by plane, others by train, there were walkabouts followed by more walkabouts, there were radio interviews, phone-ins, television interviews, inserts for the 9 o'clock news, comments for the 10 o'clock news, followed by close of play at around 11 pm on TV.

As for the back-bench MPs, they spent their days and nights scuttling round their respective constituencies throwing more and more leaflets through people's doors, talking to everyone in sight in the high street, and charging up and down in vans with loud-hailers extolling the virtues of the party's policies, and the stamina of the local candidate.

At the beginning of the campaign the Conservative Party had a substantial lead, but as the days went by it slowly began to diminish. Opinion polls appeared daily and the strains and pressures on the party leaders must have been immeasurable.

Many cynical remarks have been made about the world of politics, and politicians themselves have not been slow to comment on that extraordinarily unpredictable and unique world. As Sir Harold Wilson commented, 'A week in politics is a long time.' And there is Disraeli's 'Finality is not the language of politics' and Theodore Roosevelt's 'The most successful politician is he who says what everybody is thinking most often and in the loudest voice.'

A welcome home for Lord Soames, who played a major role in the transfer of power to Zimbabwe in 1980

Greeting the new Zimbabwe Prime Minister, Robert Mugabe, at No 10

Above: with alter ego, in wax, at Madame Tussaud's. The sculptor was Ian Hanson, for whom Mrs Thatcher sat at Downing Street; *below:* on the ball with Kevin Keegan and Emlyn Hughes prior to their leaving with the English team for the European soccer championship in Italy

Whatever may be your view, politics is not a forum for the faint-hearted, nor for those with a weak constitution.

Dawn broke on what promised to be one of the most dramatic election days the nation had witnessed. It was the day which many felt would mark a fundamental turning point in our history. Amid the sunshine and showers, people turned out in droves to register their vote. The party workers who had played such a vital part in the campaign were active from dawn to dusk chauffering the disabled, the elderly and those without transport to the polling stations. From 7 am in the morning to 10 pm at night, when the last votes were cast, the country was a hive of industry, then came the long and agonising wait while the votes were counted.

All over the land people gathered round their radio and television sets. Was Margaret Thatcher going to be the first woman in Western Europe to become Prime Minister, or were her hopes and dreams going to fade into the night? The tension mounted. . . . As the first results were declared at around midnight the atmosphere was alive with feverish anticipation. The early returns showed a swing to the Conservative Party: broad smiles appeared on the faces of their supporters, while the Labour Party followers looked disconsolate and anxious. But the outcome was still very much in the balance and no one could predict with any degree of certainty who would emerge as the victor.

It wasn't until the early hours of the morning on 4th May that Margaret Thatcher could heave a great sigh of relief. She had won a decisive victory. The Conservative Party had achieved an overall majority of 44 seats in the House of Commons, assuring Mrs Thatcher of a full five-year parliamentary term, which could be curtailed only by the extremely unlikely occurrence of a major revolt by her own backbenchers. There was a difference of two million votes between the two major parties the greatest difference since the General Election of 1935 when Stanley Baldwin led the Conservatives to victory.

To the dismay of the Socialists, the Tories had succeeded in obtaining an even greater share of the popular vote than that achieved by the Labour Party in its famous landslide victory of 1945. The electorate had given Mrs Thatcher an overwhelming vote of confidence. They had placed their faith and trust in 'The Iron Lady' and were prepared to give her a chance to write the pages of history. This, then, was the woman of whom *The Economist* had said during the battle for the Conservative Leadership: 'Her victory could keep the Conservative Party in opposition for the next twenty years.'

At the Conservative Party headquarters a jubilant Mrs Thatcher with her husband Denis and her son Mark waved to the Press and everybody else in sight.

'Aren't you tired?' enquired an exhausted reporter.

'We're not in the least bit tired,' she replied exuberantly. 'We don't think we'll ever go home!'

A smiling, triumphant Margaret Thatcher appeared on the front pages of all the national newspapers and details of the dramatic night's events filled the columns. Whenever there's a winner there must always be a loser and in the early morning a dispirited and sorely disappointed Mr Callaghan tendered his resignation to the Queen. Then, under the glaring television lights at Transport House, he said: 'I would want to congratulate Mrs Thatcher on becoming Prime Minister. It's a great office and a wonderful privilege, and for a woman to occupy that office, is I think, a tremendous moment in the country's history.

'Therefore everybody must, on behalf of all our people, wish her well and wish her success in the great responsibilities that now fall to her. She will need health, she will need strength, she will need stamina, she will need a lot of support.

'The new Government is entitled to a fair show on its voyage. It has got plenty of difficulties to overcome without us unnecessarily adding to them by factional opposition.'

Eventually, at 4 am in the morning, an elated Margaret Thatcher, flushed with the success of her historic triumph, returned to her house in Chelsea to snatch a few hours' sleep. After only three hours, her batteries recharged, she prepared herself for the day's ceremonies. Friday, 4th May was indeed a magical day for Margaret. Outside her home a large crowd had been waiting since early dawn to wish her good luck and God speed for the difficult and hazardous journey which lay ahead. She went outside to greet them looking relaxed and radiant, and her eyes glowed with pleasure as bouquets of flowers were enthusiastically showered upon her – a gesture which will surely remain imprinted on her memory for the rest of her life. For despite all the male chauvenistic posturing, despite all the criticisms of her voice, despite all the criticisms she had been subjected to simply because she was a woman, despite everything, that day Margaret Thatcher knew she had made it. She really was Prime Minister of Great Britain. To loud cheers she was driven away via Buckingham Palace to No 10 Downing Street, where another throng of cheering, waving supporters and well-wishers lined the street.

As she stood on the steps of No 10 she gave this promise: 'I shall strive unceasingly to try to fulfil the trust and confidence the British people have put in me. Now there is work to be done!'

Perhaps at this moment it is interesting to recall what she had said in an interview given to Michael Cockerell of BBC Television's Panorama, which was recorded during the election campaign. Asked whether she had any doubts at all about her ability to measure up to the job of Prime Minister, she replied in this way: 'Of course you have doubts – of course you have doubts – and you're tremendously aware of the responsibility, but I haven't just come to this out of the blue. I've been in politics for thirty years now. In British politics you don't just go from the bottom to the top – you climb your way up the ladder. I just hope that people will take me as I am for what I can do, not as a man or woman but as a personality who has an absolute passion for getting things right for Britain! I just can't bear Britain in decline . . . we who either defeated or rescued half Europe, who kept half Europe free when otherwise it would be in chains. . . . Look at us now. I just hope they'll look at that and say "Does it really matter whether

195

it's a man or woman, isn't it just better to get things right?" '

10

Face to Face

My initial visit to 10 Downing Street took place five days after Margaret Thatcher's memorable Conservative conference at Blackpool where the delegates gave Britain's first female Prime Minister an ecstatic welcome.

I arrived in good time to be greeted most hospitably by the security staff and was shown into the elegantly furnished waiting room. A number of people were waiting and the atmosphere was decidedly tense. One gentleman in the familiar pin-stripe suit paced nervously across the floor, pausing only to open his file and gaze at the contents; seemingly bemused and undoubtedly depressed by what he saw, he resolutely quickened his pace.

My reverie was interrupted by the arrival of an immaculately uniformed official. Mr Pin-stripe, full of expectation, steeled himself for the big moment, rose to his full height and giving me a nervous smile strode purposefully towards the door. But he was politely forestalled by the official announcing that I was to precede him. Mrs Thatcher welcomed me and I began my first interview with the new Prime Minister of Britain.

Was there ever a moment during the Election campaign when you felt you might not win or did your reputed inner strength enable you to retain your faith? I'm referring particularly to the last weekend of the campaign when for the first time Labour led by just under 1 per cent.

'No, there was never such a moment. We set out positive policies. We made very few specific promises and we told people the truth. Wherever I went I found a tremendous response to what we were saying. I have always believed that the only poll that really matters is Election Day itself. I used to tell our supporters never to be euphoric about favourable polls or too depressed if they were against us. So, I repeat the answer to your question is "No", and the election result proved we were right not to be deflected from our campaign strategy.'

Were there any highlights of the campaign which have remained imprinted on your memory?

'It's all go in an election campaign – from early morning until late at night. The result is that the whole period becomes a sort of kaleidoscope. Different things come to mind from time to time. Just a few which occur – and don't forget that photographers and journalists are always wanting something new and something different – were the visit to the farm in East Anglia, the brush factory near Bristol where they gave me a giant broom to make a clean sweep, and the rush to get ready the big speeches for the mass meetings. I don't like repeating speeches, so we had to get a new one ready each time.

'Then there was the high technology factory at Milton Keynes when their special monitoring system pronounced me "fit as a fiddle". But perhaps the most memorable occasion was that great rally of Conservative trade unionists at Wembley. You will remember, because you were there. It was an inspiring sight and one I shall never forget.'

What were your first thoughts on 4th May 1979 when in the early hours of the morning you knew you were the first ever female Prime Minister in the Western world?

'You don't stop to analyse your emotions at times like that,' she said softly. 'After all, with my colleagues I had been working for a General Election victory for four years. We achieved that on 3rd May, and the next day was the start of a new chapter. As I said on the steps at No 10 that Friday afternoon, there was work to be done. We went straight in and started that work. It scarcely crossed my mind that I was the first female Prime Minister in the West. I have always thought of myself as a politician who happens to be a woman.'

How quickly did you adapt to life at Downing Street?

'Four years as Leader of the Opposition is excellent training for life in Downing Street. There are times when it might not have seemed so, but on balance I tried to make the best use of those years and I was able to broaden my experience, especially in the field of foreign affairs. That, I think, has stood me in good stead at No 10. The chief difference is that Opposition can only question and exhort, Government can talk and act. I like to get on with things, so the transition was not difficult after the frustrating years of Opposition.'

What aspect of Prime Ministerial life have you found the most difficult to become accustomed to?

'Anyone in public life finds there is very little privacy. It means that it's impossible to get away from it all even for a short time.'

Has your husband found the transition difficult?

Her face lit up. 'Oh Denis is marvellous, absolutely marvellous! It's not an easy adaptation by any means, but he goes round and does many of the things I am unable to do. He is absolutely wonderful – wonderful!'

Presumably even today at Downing Street and Chequers the general working conditions are a facet of a Prime Minister's life of which few people have an real appreciation?

'In a way I suppose I've come full circle. As a girl we lived "over the shop" in Grantham, and that's the case again at No 10 now. I think there are considerable advantages in having the office and home together, but it's important to keep them in separate compartments. While I take work into the flat, which is at the top of the building, I always have meetings in the working rooms. In addition there are the State Rooms for official entertaining and meetings. Chequers offers the chance of a change of scenery and a breath of fresh air. For all that, it remains a fully operational office and is manned at all times.'

Mark said,'As a family we will have to make more sacrifices, to forego more family life, if my mother becomes Prime Minister. But I will happily pay the price.' Can you still have a private life despite the enormous pressures of public office?

'Yes, though it's true to say I have very little private life – but that little is very precious. At Christmas the family was all together – and it was wonderful. Carol is now working as a political journalist in Australia and Mark's work takes him to many different parts of the world, but we all make the effort to keep in touch regularly, usually by phone. That is my only luxury.'

Is the workload of a Prime Minister far greater than that of Leader of the Opposition? Do you find it difficult to cope or is the key prerequisite 'organisation'?

'No, I don't find any difficulty in coping with the physical strain – but then I've always been used to working hard. Indeed, I don't know what I would do without work! A methodical mind does help. I suppose that's where my legal and scientific training come in – as well as running a home.'

But while you are well known for your infinite reserves of energy, presumably there are occasions when you are overcome by tiredness?

'Well, not while there is a job of work to be done. It's when you stop that you realise you might be rather tired.'

Winston Churchill was famous for his 'cat-naps'.

'Oh, if it's possible, I can perfectly easily have a nap for ten or fifteen minutes and feel very refreshed, and I can happily sleep in the back of the car when we're travelling from one place to another.'

It has frequently been said that your aides despair of your habit of working round the clock. Do you expect them to work comparable hours?

'Only when something has to be ready for the next day,' she stressed.

Henry James, your former Press Secretary, is quoted as saying 'It's impossible to get Mrs Thatcher to relax. If she has an afternoon off she will say, "But what am I going to do with it?" Bearing this in mind, is your work your relaxation?

'Relaxation isn't quite the right word. It's the way I live. I would like to pack each minute with "sixty seconds worth of distance run".'

It is assumed that your approach to Prime Minister's Question Time is entirely different from the one you adopted as Leader of the Opposition.

'Yes – it has to be. Finding the right answer is quite

different from finding the right question. And then, you never know what the Questions are going to be. So you have to do a lot of work beforehand to try to see that you aren't taken by surprise.'

Have you noticed any significant change in Mr Callaghan in his role as Leader of the Opposition? Do you feel that his confidence has diminished?

'I don't think I'm the best person to make a judgment. What I do know is that having taken part in Question Time from both Despatch Boxes I know which I prefer every time – that's the Government side!'

In your first conference speech as Prime Minister you said: 'We want the greatest possible co-operation with both sides of industry but national policy is the sole responsibility of Government and Parliament.' How difficult will it be to get the co-operation of the unions, bearing in mind that in the years of Labour Government they have become accustomed to playing an ever-increasing role in the formulation of Government policy?

'Our standard of living depends on what we earn. Anyone who tries to increase his pay, not by earning more but by industrial muscle, does so at the expense of his fellow-citizens. It is *they* and not governments who pay the price. It is this truth that we have to drive home. Unions have a very big role to play in industrial relations. Only they, management and the employer can work things out in industry. Parliament, on the other hand, represents *all* the people, of which unions are a part.'

In the same speech you stated 'the task our Government is facing is the most difficult and the most challenging that has faced any administration since the war.'

'For years people have become used to turning to governments for the answer to their problems. rather too many people have done that. Whether they want a job, a house, a pension, more money – they say that government must provide it. But governments don't create wealth – they can only take it from the people who do. Consequently governments have overspent, overtaxed, over-borrowed and over-interfered. The result was decline because people don't work to improve the lot of government but to provide a better life for their families. For that purpose they need to keep more of their own earnings and make more of their own decisions. They want more freedom to exercise their own responsibilities. This means a great change in attitude but I believe it is the only way.'

If Labour had won the Election they would obviously have been forced to make spending cuts. Joel Barnett has admitted to that reality. Could they have chosen different options? Could the axe have fallen upon different areas of Government spending?

'They didn't win the Election, so I think it would be idle of me to speculate on what they might have done. What I do know is that on their projected spending plans it would have meant an 8p increase in income tax or VAT up to 22p in the pound. No government can escape reality for long. Eventually the last one had to call in the IMF and the spending cuts *were* made.'

Your opponents and certain sections of the media are systematically trying to destroy all your efforts to show that the Conservative Party is a caring Party. Almost daily they manage to single out a spending cut which results in the closure of a hospital, an old people's home, a home for the disabled or the mentally handicapped. How will you counteract this insidious propaganda?

'There is a lot of waste that still needs cutting out. I think precious little of any authority that would rather close down a hospital ward or nursery school than cut down on administrative staff. No one, least of all myself, wants any economies on those things which desperately ill people need. The efficiency of a service does not always increase with increasing numbers employed in it. Sometimes too many cooks spoil the broth.

'Wanting to care is not enough. You need the means to do it. The countries with the best pensions and welfare systems are those who are more successful in industry and commerce than we are.'

You declared 'we must create a wholly new attitude of mind. We must be prepared to look at things in a completely different way.' How will you persuade the British people to charter a new course?

'There is no simple magic wand to solve this problem. Example is always better than precept. If as a Government we show that we are determined to live within our means and we pursue that course steadfastly, others will follow because they *know* it makes sense.'

How do you intend to secure the trust of the British people who have become very suspicious of politicians over the years? They feel that they have been let down on a sea of broken promises. How can you restore their faith?

'We must go on telling people the facts of economic life. We didn't make a lot of promises at the Election, but some of those we did make have already been fulfilled, like increasing the pay of the police and the armed forces. Performance is better than promise. If we can achieve that, then a lot of the cynicism that has developed will disappear. There are some things that will take quite a long time because they involve a change of attitude. Those are the things we must stick at until success is achieved.'

Surely any government has a responsibility to explain to the electorate the reasons behind the actions they are taking rather than simply presenting them as a *fait accompli*. Isn't it in the field of communication where British politics has in the past been found severly lacking?

'Yes, I agree. It's not enough to do the right things; you have to explain what you are doing and why. But it is very time-consuming and we haven't, as yet, struck the right balance.'

It can be argued that politicians and the media have been prophesying doom and economic disaster for so long that people have become almost reconciled to assuming that there is no escape from our decline both as a world power and an industrial force. Once you said 'we must rekindle the spirit which years of Socialism have all but exhausted.' Given that attitude, how can the spirit of adventure, ambition and pride in our nation be rekindled?

'I can only give people the opportunity by creating tax incentives and reducing Government interference. Once those things are done, I believe that a lot of people will respond, and they will build our industrial and commercial greatness in the future. As for pride in our country – we have never lost that and never will.'

How do you react to Mr Callaghan's statement, echoed by his senior Shadow Ministers and Trade Union leaders, that 'this Tory Government is the most reactionary Government since the war?

'Well – there was a lot to react against and the time had come to do it!'

You have frequently warned that 'if you turn your back on new technology, you turn your back on your own future.' So many unions rebel against the use of new technology. How can they be persuaded to use new equipment and to create tomorrow's jobs rather than constantly trying to protect yesterday's?

'This is a matter of patient persuasion and of showing that successful nations have done just that. Without change many jobs will be lost forever as other nations forge ahead. Innovation and inventiveness have long been British characteristics. It's those men of ideas and talent whom we must encourage. It is to *them* we must look for tomorrow's jobs. And in their hearts Trade Unionists know it.'

Was it to some extent an emotional decision to go to Northern Ireland after the murder of Lord Mountbatten, and the horrific killing of so many British soldiers? Did you stop to think about the great personal danger?

Her voice lowered. 'I just felt I should go and so I went. I'm glad I did.'

The Commonwealth Conference in Zambia promised to be a somewhat unnerving and harrowing experience for Britain's Prime Minister. For a well-orchestrated violent anti-Thatcher campaign awaited her arrival in Lusaka. During the flight in the RAF VC-10, Lord Carrington, who was sitting behind the PM, noticed a pair of sunglasses with huge lenses on her lap. Observing his enquiring glance, she said 'I've taken these in case they get rough and throw acid in my face.'

The plane touched down at Lusaka airport amidst a

pandemonium of chanting, seemingly hostile black faces. The doors of the plane opened and the intense heat of the African night engulfed the aircraft. The Prime Minister rose from her seat and without a backward glance walked resolutely down the steps into the waiting jostling throng. the sunglasses remained on the plane. Everyone in the British party were impressed, not least the Foreign Secretary, Lord Carrington. But how had Margaret Thatcher felt in that climate of antagonism, which had been fermenting for some time? How had she ultimately won the respect and trust of the African delegates?

'It wasn't very nice,' she said quietly. 'So many horrid and untrue things were being written. But we overcame them because they were patently false. The Conference lasted for some eight days so there was plenty of time to talk things over.'

You described the Election result as a victory for conviction and commitment. You have described yourself as a conviction politician. How would you interpret your main convictions?

'Goodness, there's enough in that question on which to write a book! Perhaps the best summary is to be found in the sayings attributed to Abraham Lincoln.' She reached for a book and turned up the relevant reference:

> You cannot bring about prosperity by discouraging thrift.
> You cannot strengthen the weak by weakening the strong.
> You cannot help strong men by tearing down big men.
> You cannot help the wage-earner by pulling down the wage-payer.
> You cannot further the brotherhood of man by encouraging class hatred.
> You cannot help the poor by destroying the rich.
> You cannot establish sound security on borrowed money.
> You cannot keep out of trouble by spending more than you earn.
> You cannot build character and courage by taking

away man's initiative and independence.
You cannot help men permanently by doing for them what they could and should do for themselves.

My final interview with Mrs Thatcher took place in the summer of 1980 at Downing Street.

Do you feel you have changed since you became Prime Minister?

'Well, I have no idea but other people say I have. Not within myself. In so far as personal relationships are concerned, not at all. I don't think Denis feels that I have changed in any way – he always sees the same side. But I suppose that the volume of work one has to do is so very great that you give the appearance of being much more decisive and much more definite. It isn't that one lacked decision before, but the sheer volume makes everything appear more positive and brisk.'

Several observers have alluded to your rising air of confidence as Prime Minister. They have particularly emphasised your steadily growing dominance during proceedings and debates in the House of Commons.

'I think when you have learned to do a job, you are always more confident after you have handled it for some time than you were at the very beginning. It's the same with any new job.'

Do you suffer from tension?

'No, I don't become tense, but I do feel very strongly about certain issues, therefore one is inclined to give them total concentration to the exclusion of all else. For example, when we were in Luxembourg negotiating Britain's contributions to the EEC we started at 10 o'clock in the morning and dispersed at about 10.30 in the evening. One had absolutely total concentration during the whole of that period.'

The majority of people appear to find speechmaking an essentially unnerving experience, How do you react before a major speech?

'Well, I'm always nervous, tense in that sense . . . yes, always. As you're obliged to make a fair amount of speeches you can never be on top form the whole time, consequently, you are always rather tense. Sometimes you have to make them when there are many other things on your mind, but nevertheless you have to erase them from your mind and suddenly swing into a speech.'

Do you feel you are more relaxed and less tense now as Prime Minister than you were as Leader of the Opposition?

'I honestly don't know . . . it's just a different job. It's a very different job. In a way, you have more support as Prime Minister because the moment you become PM far more of the routine tasks are carried out for you, tasks which as Leader of the Opposition, you were obliged to cope with yourself. But you are busy in a different way. For instance, you do very much more in the field of foreign affairs. When I was in Opposition I used to think I was pretty involved in that sphere: I made several trips abroad and saw many overseas dignitaries in London. However, a larger proportion of your time is devoted to foreign affairs when you are Prime Minister than is the case when you are Leader of the Opposition.

'Woman is a belated survival from a primeval age of struggle and competition; that is why, the world over, you find all the superfluous dust and worry being made by the gentler sex.'

Is Margaret Thatcher a natural worrier?

'Oh, I always worry about the children, always. When Mark is racing I obviously worry a great deal, but I try to tell myself that no news is good news. I don't worry about the little things. For many years now I simply haven't had the time . . . I suppose I have so many big issues to concern myself with, and then I worry in the sense of puzzling away at them. But, yes, I'm always anxious and apprehensive about my family. Always!'

Do the affairs of State involve sleepless nights?

'Sometimes, if you have something very very important to do the following day, the problem simply won't go away; your mind goes on working and working and you just lie awake.'

Have you any particular fear?

'I can't think of one at all . . .' She paused for several moments, looking pensive. 'I'm not afraid of flying, or hospitals . . . or dying . . . No, I really can't think of anything at all.'

Does it anger you if people frequently change their minds on important issues, or when under public examination fail to have the courage of their convictions?

She became absorbed in thought and said slowly but resolutely, 'I don't like it if people say one thing in private and another in public. They must say the same thing on both occasions.'

Despite your Government's persistent warnings of the perilous effects of high wages unmatched by a commensurate increase in output, productivity in this country still remains at a dismally low level. How can you prevent people from pricing themselves and their fellow-workers out of the labour market? How many people must lose their jobs before reality takes over from insanity?

'You have enormous variations now from factory to factory, from group to group and from office to office. In some of the small businesses the output is stupendous, the performance is marvellous – they are working flat out! No such things as restrictive practices. It is in some of the very much larger concerns where you encounter restrictive practices and over-manning. All I can say is they have enormous scope for improvement if *only* they will take it. But certainly some of them are much more realistic – British Leyland is a very good example. The workforce accepted considerably less because they knew their future was in jeopardy. The ship-building industry settled for a great deal less, too, and many smaller companies have adopted the same realistic approach.

'When I went to the Birmingham Chamber of Commerce and Industry, they said, "Look, you don't hear about the claims which are being settled for very much less, but quite a number do settle for less because the workers realise their future is at stake." And that is the message I'm urgently trying to get across! If you take too

208

much the goods will be too highly priced, consequently the order books will be empty and the whole firm will be forced to close down. That is what one is desperately trying to preach and it is *going to come true*. If they do take too much the level of unemployment will rise. If they exact wage settlements at an inflated level a company will have insufficient funds to finance moden technology, with the inevitable result that the firm will fall behind and be overtaken by their competitors. But, sadly, on occasions the message has to be learned by experience. It's a tragedy really . . . a tragedy!'

How do you overcome the complexities of the essential nationalised industries?

'It's very difficult, very difficult. We haven't solved that dilemma as yet because they are monopolies and they do pose a threat. They can hold the nation to ransom. It is one of the greatest problems, and of course their prices have risen more steeply than any others. Nationalised industries, any monopolies, are bad for the consumer, but they are, in fact, the legacy of Socialism which set out to create State monopolies in the belief they would work better for the consumer,. but that simply isn't the case: their hopes haven't been realised – it just hasn't happened that way. Competition serves the people very much better than monopolies!'

Unemployment is a highly sensitive and emotive political issue. While it is conceded that unemployment is a crucial and difficult problem throughout the majority of the industrialised nations, many of your critics allege that rising unemployment is a direct result of your hard-line policies.

'Don't forget, under the last Labour Government unemployment went up enormously, it rose from 600,000 to one and a half million. Then they created an artificial boom, and when you have a boom of that nature it's *always* followed by inflation the following year – that is what we are suffering from now. Furthermore, the increase in the price of oil has added five per centage points to the Retail Price Index. Now the last Labour

209

Government didn't have to cope with this serious problem, because the price of oil didn't rise while they were in office; in fact, in real terms the price actually went down; yet under their stewardship unemployment still rose to one and a half million. Last year, as a result of the Iranian crisis, the price of oil rose by 100 per cent, which is a fantastic increase, so you can appreciate the sort of problems confronting us.

'Over-manning is another factor. There's far too much over-manning, a main contributor to making Britain uncompetitive. Steel is a prime example. We've had to import steel because our own industry was pricing itself out of the home market. People are under the misconception that over-manning saves jobs. I'm afraid the reverse is true, it doesn't it leads to the loss of jobs. If an industry is run economically business will thrive, if it isn't you will lose business and customers will go to alternative sources. If the steel industry had been run economically we could have retained more of the home market.

'Many people have good jobs. Every time they go on prolonged strikes they put their jobs and those of their fellow-workers in jeopardy. One of the causes of unemployment is prolonged strikes. That is the reality we must drive home. We have given incentives, to people, we are reducing government spending, we shall bring down inflation; how successful we are on unemployment will depend upon people's response. But more and more people are responding, more and more people are refusing to go on strike, more and more people *are* facing the realities.'

If the Labour Party had been returned to power, do you think there would have been a similar rise in the rate of inflation?

'Oh, they would have had exactly the same problems. The incomes policy had broken down and what Mr Callaghan did at the end of that period was to say "all right, take nine per cent now and go to Clegg." ' It has fallen to us to pick up the tab from all the Clegg recommendations. Indeed, they might have had even more problems, because they wouldn't, in my view, have cut

210

back on the money supply. It's a basic principle that if you start solving problems by printing money then that leads to inflation. In essence, inflation is the amount of money in the system which is not backed by goods and services.'

While emphasising your strengths in certain spheres, Lord George-Brown contended that it was in the field of industry where you lacked both knowledge and experience. 'I don't think Margaret Thatcher knows very much about industry,' he commented.

'Oh, how absurd,' she said quietly. 'I worked in industry. Denis has been in industry all his life – he has a lifetime's experience of it – and we often discuss industrial problems together. I think I have probably been closer to industry in practice than most other politicians; very few have actually worked in industry as I have. . . . I don't agree with George at all.'

It has been alleged that during Cabinet or other meetings people have to assert their own point of view very strongly for fear of it not being heard.

'Oh no, if they want to speak, they can speak. I always look around to see whether anyone else wants to say anything.'

But presumably it's essential to be fully cognisant of the facts?

'If they want to talk about something they should have their facts clear. . . yes.'

The hierarchy of the Trade Unions is almost entirely male-dominated. Bearing this in mind, is it more difficult for you as a female Prime Minister to communicate with them? Do you feel it creates a conscious or even unconscious barrier. Are they perhaps inhibited in their discussions since they are unaccustomed to negotiating with a woman?

'Negotiations are between employers and employees. Only rarely is government in the role of employer – ie the Civil Service, the Armed Forces, etc – and then there is well-established machinery for negotiations. From time to time I meet both the CBI and TUC and find no

211

difficulty in saying what I want to say, or in understanding them. I always enjoy discussing things of mutual interest.'

Do you feel they are as open and frank in discussion with you as they presumably were with your predecessor, or do you think they regard you as an enemy of the Trade Union movement?

'I think they put just exactly the same views to me as they did to Mr Callaghan. The difficulty is that the Trade Unions finance the Labour Party: their views are identical. They exacted a price for an incomes policy which was more nationalisation, more Trade Union legislation, more public expenditure. And it is no earthly good them coming to me with the same recipe because it is that which landed this country in the winter of discontent, in heavy inflation, more nationalisation, more Trade Union law, and finally into the hands of the IMF. And so the difficulty is that the leaders of Trade Unions espouse totally the comparatively Left-Wing Labour cause. Well, I don't! If they came to talk about the practical problems of industry it would be very different, but I don't think there is any difference in what they actually say to me as opposed to what they probably would have said to Mr Callaghan.

'For my part I say: "Look, my job is politics and when you come to talk to me I don't expect to enter into a discussion about politics, about political decisions, because I take those decisions in Government and I am responsible to Parliament." I expect to talk about the real practical problems of how we are going to increase output per person, how we are going to eradicate restrictive practices, how we are going to keep more competitive, how we are going to be able to sell against countries like Germany, Japan, France and the United States; because at the present time our competition is not emanating from the low-cost countries, it is coming from the high wage countries. Those are the practical considerations. As long as they talk to me about industrial relations we will get on extremely well together. The Trade Unions have an enormous contribution to make if only they would make it!'

212

Since those far off days of 1975, when the Referendum results showed a majority in favour of Britain's entry into the EEC, the feelings of disillusionment and disenchantment have grown with the passing of every year. We were told that membership of the Community would lead to a new spirit of unity and co-operation between the Western allies – the evidence so far has been to the contrary. Far from the long-awaited, passionately hoped for harmony, we have experienced dissension and discord on a wide range of vitally important economic issues.

'Well, yes; within the Community we do have disagreements, but when it comes to a major foreign affairs issue, on the whole we have stood together... except, of course, on the Olympics where regrettably Germany was the only member country which stood with the United States. However, the Governments all stood together; it was the various Olympic committees which opposed the boycott of the Moscow games. But on the crucial statements on Afghanistan and the American hostages, we gave each other total support – we were all of one accord, so the internal disagreements have not affected the major international issues.'

But it would appear that there have been no tangible advantages. I would suggest that the idealist's dream has become the pessimist's nightmare, that in almost every sphere Britain has been disadvantaged by her decision to join the community.

'No, I don't think that's true. Firstly, the nine countries do come together to discuss foreign affairs by virtue of being members of the Community, and that is the single most important and overriding factor. Secondly, in fact our exports to the Common Market have increased; all right, I concede that their exports to Britain have grown, but 42 per cent of our exports now go to the Common Market countries. That would not have occurred if we had been outside the EEC because we would have been obliged to go through a tariff barrier. Thirdly, many overseas companies will consider investing in this country because it represents a way into the Common Market and

213

they would not necessarily invest here if we were outside the Community.

'In many cases we simply haven't taken full advantage of our opportunities. There is no earthly reason why we shouldn't be supreme engineers and challenge the Germans on many of the things they produce. We do, in fact, export a fair amount of machinery to Germany but they have opted to specialise in some of the more sophisticated machinery and we really ought to be in that market – we could be! We import a lot of textiles from Italy; they're certainly not cheap, they are expensive. Why do people buy them? Because they have the merit of quality, design, and prompt delivery. But, you know, we spend a small fortune on our art and design schools, we have many super designers and there is no reason in the world why we shouldn't do just as well as our competitors.

'Look at the car industry. The biggest import from the Common Market is cars. That is the fault of our manufacturers, the opportunity was there, but it's up to us to take full advantage of those opportunities!

'But let us for a moment look beyond the realms of industry. It's my belief that we are gradually gravitating towards more concerted action on the major international problems, and in the last analysis it is that factor which will ultimately keep the peace of the world. For that reason I think membership of the Community is a good thing.'

The new Left is deemed to consist of a consortium of Marxists, Trotskyites, Leninists, Maoists and various groups such as the Socialist Workers Party and the Anti-Nazi League. It would appear that their objective is to perpetrate the total disruption of industry, which will inexorably lead to economic disaster of cataclysmic proportions. It is their belief, or so one assumes, that by this method the democratically elected Government would be completely undermined, capitalism would be put under insurmountable pressures and the power of the new 'Left' would be born out of chaos and disaster. Your policies are pure anathema to the Left. If the militants took to the

214

streets to protest about your proposals for Trade Union reform, how would you react in what would be an unprecedented situation in this country?

'Oh I think we would cope and it would be essential for us to stand absolutely firm. I think the people themselves would cope. There is no sympathy with these militants whatsoever. You have only to recall the disgust aroused in the minds of the public by some of the violent picketing scenes. Now the police have coped with the worst of the picketing because they have a Government which is absolutely behind them, a Government which says, "We are just not going to stand for this form of protest, people have a right to be able to go to work." The police know we are resolutely behind them in law and order. There's nothing political about it in any way. The police are non-political and must always remain so.

'I will not countenance people saying to me, "if you do what ought to done, then we'll have industrial trouble." I'm going on steadily to implement those measures which I believe are necessary for the success and prosperity of Britain, and I'm going to rely on the common-sense of the British people, including those in Trade Unions, to back me. For the people who are asking us most vigorously for these reforms are members of the Trade Unions themselves who recognise that some of the practices taking place at the present time are absurd – they don't want to take part in them but they are afraid of the resulting consequences as the provisions of the law now stand.

It's my firm belief there is no public sympathy with these militants at all and *together* we are going to beat the militants and the wreckers!'

A great deal of attention has been focused upon the decline of the West, on its economic instability and on the disintegration of its social fabric. But how many people in the West would willingly choose to spend their lives in the 'land of the dissidents'. Is there any country in the world where, in your view, the people have benefited from Socialist policies?

'I can't think of any developed country in the world

which has really benefited from Socialist policies. Russia most certainly hasn't, and that is where they are found in their most extreme form. To take another example, in pre-war days Czechoslovakia was one of the most prosperous countries in Europe. She becomes a member of the Communist Socialist bloc and as a result she no longer enjoys the prosperity she once had. A free society undoubtedly produces a much higher standard of living. I suppose China is the only successful Communist-Socialist country, because they have a Government that has got things organised. They are becoming a freer society and now realise that the creation of incentives is the only way to get increased production.'

During the course of conversation with Patrick Cosgrave in 1976, in which you were apparently discussing the direction and approach of the Conservative Party, you are reputed to have said, 'I have changed everything.' Several political observers have focused attention upon this statement and have made somewhat varying interpretations as to its meaning.

Margaret Thatcher looked slightly puzzled and paused to reflect for several moments. 'I'm sorry,' she said, 'but this just doesn't ring a bell with me at all. . . . I certainly think if it had any meaning at all it meant that we have, in fact, got things on to a consistent basis, in that we believe in certain specific principles which will accordingly give rise to certain policies and that we will pursue those policies so that everthing is consistent.

'If we have changed our approach it was right away from the idea that politics is just dealing with things as they arise on the basis of expediency. We are working towards a specific objective, a specific way of life, trying to eradicate many many old attitudes, trying fundamentally to reform a number of things, trying to get a capital-owning democracy so that everyone, no matter what their background, has some chance to own some property, to accumulate some savings. This is quite a change, everyone, whatever their background, has the chance to rise to the limits of their ability, because on the whole a people develop by two things: firstly by encouraging the extremely talented among them, and secondly by having the back-up of the vast majority of the population – working, understanding, that freedom means responsibility. We believe in a way of life that will help people to climb the ladder by their own efforts and which will help the unfortunate when they stumble.'

The Civil Service is an immensely powerful organization. There are many talented and able people within its ranks, and it's inescapably true that the civil servants have a distinct advantage over any incoming government. For the minister's role is transient, the civil servant's permanent. Perhaps with this truism in mind it was predicted that Margaret Thatcher would become the prisoner of the dictates of the mandarins of Whitehall like many of her predecessors. As yet, the evidence has disproved that prediction. How has she succeeded in that sphere where so many others had seemingly failed?

'I think it's simply a question of having very fierce, very strong beliefs, and perhaps it can also be attributed to the fact that Whitehall isn't used to dealing with a woman Prime Minister. In that sense it's an advantage being a woman. In my job you mustn't become the prisoner of anyone, but you must be approachable by everyone. There is, of course, no point in being here unless you have strong beliefs and are determined to put them into action. That's what I was elected to do.'

According to rumours circulating in Whitehall, some members of the Civil Service are decidedly terrified of you. The PM seemed to be highly amused by this remark and began to laugh.

'Are they? Oh!' she said, still laughing. 'Well my own staff certainly aren't, and we all work together marvellously. I think we all enjoy it,' she said vigorously as she leant towards me. 'It's exciting! It's stimulating! We don't just wait for things to happen, we *make* them happen!'

According to widely disseminated reports you have taken the unprecedented step of visiting various departments of the Civil Service, a practice unexplored by your predecessors.

'Yes, that's right – no Prime Minister has ever carried out that practice. I go and see what's happening. I go to see the people who are making it happen!'

Perhaps that strikes a certain wariness in their hearts?

'Maybe. . . maybe. Actually, you find we have a tremendous amount of really able young people in the Civil Service and I don't think we use their talents enough. It takes them a long time to get to the top. We have a lot of able youngsters, really able youngsters, and in my view they are not always being used to the full limit of their ability.'

According to some observers, it would appear that you have experienced a sense of frustration in the office of Prime Minister, that your consummate desire to forge ahead on certain key issues has, to some extent, been thwarted by political exigencies.

'Well, you have to remember that a democracy consists of moving ahead by persuasion. You have a Cabinet of about twenty-two and while you all know exactly what you want to do and the goals you are pledged to achieve, sometimes there are differences about just how fast you can go. It is in that area where you get the debate, and sometimes I think we can go faster, I think we *must push,* we must push ahead, and then suddenly you realise that perhaps you are going too fast for people to absorb all at once – so that is the area in which there is most debate.

'Frustrating? Sometimes, I find it personally frustrating in that I would like to proceed at a greater pace on one or two issues. There are certain instances which really are frustrating – interest rates, for example. You know how much I hated having to put interest rates up: that was because too many people were borrowing. There were more people wanting to borrow than there were people wanting to save. Government was borrowing, manufacturing industry was borrowing heavily, personal-sector borrowing was fairly high – so basically there was just too much borrowing in the system as compared with the amount of saving – there was a shortage of savings. Con-

218

sequently the price of borrowing had to go up and I had hoped to have brought it down before now. All we can do as a Government is to try to pull out of borrowing which means cutting down our own spending. You are right, it is frustrating, it does take longer than you think! [The interest rate was subsequently cut.].

'Another frustrating aspect concerns the size of the bureaucracies. We are constantly told that the bureaucracies are too large and it does take longer than you think to cut them down, particularly if you are working on a policy in which I believe – nil redundancies; but that sometimes means you have to have nil recruitment, because you really can't operate a policy which puts people in fear of losing their job in the Civil Service.

'Some of these things do take longer than you think and I *am* impatient, if I weren't I wouldn't *drive* them on as fast as I do.'

It is reputed that one of your greatest difficulties lies in the fact that on many central issues you don't have a natural majority in your Cabinet – that the Cabinet doesn't consist of a preponderance of people who share your instinctive views of the required policies.

'Oh no! Oh no! I have got most of my things through – oh no!'

Loyalty and discretion are the reputed characteristics of previous Tory administrations, yet some commentators have claimed that your Cabinet has layed bare its internal disputes in an unprecedented manner.

'Oh I think in today's climate everything is much more open than it used to be – much more is known. That is the whole atmosphere of society; everyone wants to know everything. After all, there are a tremendous number of commentators devoted to finding out and they find out in the most skilful ways – it's just one of the natural hazards of life.'

But are discussions in Cabinet under your leadership particularly open and forthright?

'Well, certainly I run it in the sense that I don't want a lot of people in the Cabinet who are just flatterers or just

219

rubber stamps. We do come to conclusions by *argument*, and very good argument it is too.'

Is there any facet of the premiership which you have found particularly difficult to master?

'No. . . well not as far as I am aware. I think my critics are the people to ask about that. While it's not difficult to master, I have been surprised at the amount of time we actually have to spend on foreign affairs. The amount of summitry we have now is terrific. There are three European summits a year, there is an Economic summit each year and every alternate year a Commonwealth summit; then there are all sorts of talks between two countries. We have two sessions of talks between Germany and Britain and between Italy and Britain every year, and one session between France and Britain. We go to the United States: en route to the Economic summit I went through Moscow and on my return journey I visited Australia. So there is quite a lot of international work to be done. Fortunately, we have a great many people coming to London from all over the world and we do learn a good deal from them directly. Malcolm Fraser comes from Australia and Bob Maldoon from New Zealand, which is absolutely vital because they are such a long way away. If we didn't have these reciprocal visits we wouldn't keep in contact, and we *must.*'

As a dedicated conviction-politician anxious to put your policies into practice and impatient for results, have you been subject to more constraints than you had envisaged?

'Well, no; we are starting. We've had a massive programme of legislation this year. We have made a start on Trade Union reform, the Housing Bill has gone through, enabling people to purchase council houses and have a right to purchase council houses. It will also enable people to let rooms or small flats on a specific short lease with the certainty that they can regain possession after a fixed period of time – and it is therefore my hope that this Bill will bring more rentable property onto the market.

'We have started on a de-nationalisation programme and we really have done a tremendous amount in the way of

220

social services, which we don't always get credit for. We said to war widows: "You are not going to pay any more tax on your war widows' pension", and we have kept our promise – it was one of our very first actions. For they lost their husbands, who gave their lives so that we might live the way we do today. Additionally, we have helped widows during their first year of widowhood: it's a dreadful period, it's a period of great adjustment and, my goodness, they have enough adjustment to make emotionally without having to worry too much about finance.

'We have kept our promise by having retirement pensions rise in line with prices. In fact we are still, in real terms, spending the same amount on the National Health Service. We have taken steps to help the lower paid – there are many people who prefer to work rather than joining the ranks of the unemployed even though they earn comparatively low wages. In some instances they can find a job which gives them both dignity and respect but where the wages aren't very high. We have said to them "Rather than your having to go on the dole we will increase the family income supplement." It's much better for them to have the dignity and respect of a job. We have, really, when you think about it, done a fantastic amount in one year.'

During a conversation at a private luncheon deemed to be protected by the conventions of privilege, Mr James Prior, the Employment Minister, cast certain aspersions on the capabilities of the then Chairman of British Steel, Sir Charles Villiers. These remarks proved to be a source of embarrassment to the PM, Sir Charles Villiers and Mr Prior himself. When interviewed on BBC's Panorama Mrs Thatcher was asked by Robin Day why she hadn't sacked Mr Prior for his apparent indiscretions, to which she replied, 'Good heavens, if you're going to kick up a terrible fuss over one mistake it doesn't really seem to be fair does it? We all make mistakes now and then. I think it was a mistake and Jim Prior was very very sorry indeed for it; very apologetic. But you don't just sack a chap for one mistake.'

221

Mr Prior is purported to have been somewhat angered by this public admonishment. The PM considered it to be an act of forgiveness, but some critics contend Mrs Thatcher neither forgives nor forgets.

'Ooh, neither forgives nor forgets,' she repeated the words thoughtfully. 'You tend not to forget just because you have a good memory, but you *do* forgive, things recede, things don't matter so much. You can't live your life by harbouring grudges against people; life's too short and it would show in your face, and in your attitude.'

Sir Geoffrey Howe felt you would not lightly forgive disloyalty.

'Well I believe you should be loyal to the things which put you in power – *totally loyal!* – I couldn't bear disloyalty to those things at all because that would be tantamount to getting in on a false prospectus.'

How would you answere the many people who voted for you in the last election, some breaking the habit of a generation, if not of a lifetime, who now claim that you promised more stringent measures in two particular spheres, namely Trade Union reform and immigration control?

'We're only in the first year. We are taking action on secondary picketing, we are doing most of the things in the manifesto, though not quite all. I agree we have not yet implemented all the promises contained in the manifesto, but we have only been in power for just over a year.'

While acknowledging that you are still in the early stages of your term of office, do you not sense a feeling of disappointment among certain sections of the electorate?

'No, though I think many people would have been prepared to have gone further than we have in this first Bill. But we are only talking about one year; it is, after all, a programme for a five-year Parliament. But don't think it is one bill and finish. There are a lot of other consider-ations, and we shall be putting forward some ideas in what is called a green paper. It is a continuing process – a progression. By the time we get to the next election we are duty-bound to have honoured all the pledges in our

222

manifesto.'

So people won't be disappointed at the end of the day?

'I hope not,' said the PM with a wry smile.

Prior to the Election, the Conservative Party gave assurances that they would severely cut the number of immigrants coming into the country and 'hold out a clear prospect of an end to immigration'. They further promised to set up a register of dependants, introduce a quota system and draw up a new British Nationality Act. When the new rules on immigration were announced in Parliament commentators most sympathetic to your cause were almost unanimous in their view that the proposals had been considerably watered down.

'No, they haven't been considerably watered down. If you look at the regulations, we were accused by some people of introducing clauses which were very tough, particularly on "fiancés" which is really where the main new immigration was coming from – and as you know, far fewer dependants are entitled to settle here now. Those regulations are through. The Nationality Bill will be introduced this year; as I say, you can't do everything at once and that will undoubtedly be a considerable undertaking. We haven't decided on whether or not to set up a register of dependants. It would be rather expensive both financially and in terms of the number of people required to operate it. As yet we have made no final decision on that issue.'

Many people who are desperately worried about rising unemployment, the housing shortage and the growing pressures on the social services, question the wisdom of any Government allowing more people into the country and thereby adding to those problems.

'Yes, I entirely agree. I accept that premise, that is why we have, in fact, cut down on immigration, we really have – and those regulations are through.'

A perceptive philosopher once said, 'Popularity is a crime from the moment it is sought; it is only a virtue where men have it whether they will or no.' While many would agree with this concept, it would be difficult to deny that the majority of the human race would wish to be well

223

thought of by their fellow-man. Did Margaret Thatcher feel the need to be popular with the electorate?

'You mustn't set out to be liked or to be popular; you must set out to do the things which you believe have to be done. Only by pursuing that course will you be acting in what you believe are the best interests of your country. Some people will take a short-term view. We *have* to take a longer-term view, but the interesting factor is that people now realise we must take a longer term view. You can't do everything on the basis of expediency because that simply leads to the situation in which we found ouselves when we were forced to go to the IMF under the last Labour Government.'

Lord George-Brown contended that you had always been subject to quite unfair special criticism simply bcause you are a woman. Do you feel this is a justified evaluation of your treatment by the media?

'No, no, I have never felt I was unfairly treated. On the whole I think I get a reasonably fair deal, and if you are in politics you must not be super-sensitive. There are people who fundamentally disagree with you and they're out to topple you. All right, so be it, that's part of our political system. If you are Prime Minister and you have had to fight your way up, as I did, you fight your way up by believing certain things, by doing certain things! If you are a very positive person you are bound to excite controversy. But there is no point in being where I am unless you want to do positive things – and all right I enjoy the controversy. And it is right that people should subject what you're doing to a critical faculty – that, too, helps sometimes; they come up with ideas you haven't thought of. The way to have an easy life is to do nothing in particular and to do it very well, but if you positively do something, then as well as making friends you will make enemies. It must not stop you doing things!'

According to a report in the *Observer*, 'After a particularly bruising encounter at No 10, one minister retired in tears to her department and had to be comforted with a glass of whisky.'

224

'I don't believe it!'

The realities of office may arouse a sense of disillusionment. Have you suffered any disappointments during your initial term?

There was a momentary pause. 'Well, if I have they can't have been very serious because they haven't lasted long. Although, as I've said, it bothered me enormously that the interest rate had to go up to 17 per cent – it really was devastating. The fact that we haven't as yet been able to turn round the rate of inflation has been a disappointment – it's taking longer to turn things round. However, in spite of all the forecasts of doom and gloom last year the actual standard of living in our first year rose by 6 per cent. In spite of the increase in prices, incomes went ahead by 6 per cent. Now some of that extra 6 per cent has come out of the profits of industry and my worry is that they haven't enough money to invest for next year. It is taking longer to turn things round than one had thought: you must get the investment in industry and the moment you get it drawn out of industry by people taking out too much in wages, then really they are living on next year's seed corn – but they are borrowing very heavily and that *is* unhealthy. I now have to say to people, "Look, the only way to turn this country round, when Government has done everything it possibly can, is for people to work more efficiently and more effectively, *and* it's essential we have fewer strikes." It is of paramount importance that I get this message home.'

Professor Friedman, one of the world's leading experts on the practice of monetarism, criticised your Government for its failure to instigate the necessary cuts in public expenditure. He claimed that you should have cut Government spending in real terms, that it wasn't enough merely to hold it at 1979 levels.

'It's a very fine balance. One wanted to go as fast as one possibly could, but when all the various programmes are actually in existence, have already been set in motion, then it does take time to actually reduce them and to reduce them in a humane way. It's my belief that if we had

225

received rather more in the way of co-operation and rather less in the way of resistance, we could have moved faster, *but* there are quite a number of people with a vested interest in high Government spending. You see, the moment you start to make cuts you are subjected to enormous pressures. All sorts of interest groups are lined up against you, urging you not to make any cuts in public expenditure. "You mustn't cut this, you mustn't cut that", they cry. But I have to say in answer to their pleas, "Look, during your own lifetime you are obliged to live within a certain income and if you are spending more than you earn you have to cut down on certain things. You may not like it but you know you've got to do it – there's no alternative." I have to do the same thing on behalf of the nation – it's my duty.'

During the war Roosevelt is reputed to have said 'Never before have we had so little time to do so much.' Is that an appropriate appraisal of your Government's task during this Parliament?

'We have a bigger turnaround to achieve in five years than anyone has ever attempted during the post war period – that's quite true. The fact that one is keeping resolute is helping the "turn round", is helping the change of attitude to take place. While I think we have done quite a lot during the first year, we must press on, there is so much more to accomplish. . . We must press on,' she repeated softly.

Most world leaders are reputed to have a mentor. Is that applicable to you?

'No, it doesn't apply to me. No'

You once said 'Being a head of Government can be rather lonely,' and one of the disadvantages of exalted political office is that you are in danger of becoming remote from public opinion, remote from the views of people you were elected to represent.

'It would be very easy to be isolated because I just can't walk down the street and pop into the supermarkets or the small retail grocers as I used to because you are stopped by so many people. I find that aspect of the premiership difficult and the only alternative is perhaps to go for walks

226

in the country where you are not stopped. However, I do make a point of going on walkabouts which gives me the opportunity of meeting and talking with all kinds of people. I also see a tremendous number of people at No 10 and as well as going to many Government and Civil Service departments I visit various parts of the country – I do go out and about wherever possible. For I know that I must *never, never, never,* see *only* one's advisers, see *only* State papers, I have to meet a wide variety of people, who represent wholly different viewpoints, who will say to me: "Look, the advice you were given is wrong, we want you to know what the situation really is." I am constantly seeing people, and new places and new things which I haven't seen before, and I love it. You only really live, as you know, when one is responding to people!

'But, yes it's rather more difficult than it was, it's inevitable, because the security is so much tighter. For example, when I was in Luxembourg for one of the EEC summits, an official car was waiting to take me back to the hotel. "Where is the hotel?" I enquired. Well it wasn't very far away, we could see it in the distance, so I told them we would walk. "No, no, no," came the reply, but I insisted on walking and we managed to escape. I think the British contingent were the only ones who did!'

Have you any disquieting doubts about your ability to succeed in making Britain prosperous again?

'I have every confidence in our policies. If we persevere with them, they will succeed. The important factor is "continuity". You cannot chop and change. That is fatal, Fatal!'

It has frequently been said that our economic problems are of such magnitude that it will take a long time for your monetarist policies to work through. You stated that in trying to reverse our economic decline 'the Government is bucking the trend of the last twenty years'. If the electorate become impatient for the trappings of success and vote your Government out of office at the next election, how would you see the future of this country?

'Oh well, we have a very very long way to go. I believe

227

our policies will be seen to have worked before the next Election, and I believe we shall have very much more self-respect as a nation. I believe even now, after only little more than a year, we have a much higher standing in the world. . . .

On her first day as Prime Minister, as she stood on the steps of No 10, Margaret Thatcher expressed the aspirations of her Government in the paraphrased words of St Francis of Assisi:

'Where there is discord, may we bring harmony

Where there is error, may we bring truth.

Where there is doubt, may we bring faith.

Where there is despair, may we bring hope.'

It is, as yet, too early to judge whether all her hopes will be realised.

Afterword

As Lord Thorneycroft has pertinently said, 'It is foolish to comment in depth about someone like Margaret Thatcher who is at the beginning of the main and important part of her career. There are no doubt desperate battles and bitter decisions which lie ahead. Public life is a hard and dangerous business and public life at the very top can be a very lonely and unforgiving situation. Mrs Thatcher brings to it great gifts and the high hopes of millions of her fellow countrymen. She is no doubt better as a Prime Minister than as a Leader of an opposition, though no mean performer in either role: to those who know her she is a woman enjoying simplicity and capable of great compassion; to the world about her she is a new hope bringing faith, a brilliant mind and a ruthless determination to the tasks which now crowd in upon her.'

Margaret Thatcher's manifest faith in the British people, in their talents and capabilities, was reciprocated by many at the last Election when they gave her party a substantial majority and a chance to invoke a radical change, both in our approach to economic policy and in our attitude towards the role of the Welfare State and the responsibility and liberty of the individual.

While it's obviously far too early to make any worthwhile judgement on the Government's performance, many of Margaret Thatcher's opponents claim that the honeymoon period is long since over, and that the electorate's belief and faith in the 'Iron Lady' has already turned sour – that disappointment and disenchantment have replaced optimism and hope.

But what is the reality? Do the people still believe? 'The truth that makes men free is for the most part the truth which men prefer not to hear.'

After years of patchwork government, of continuous

229

retreat at the prospect of public anger, disapproval or unpopularity, after years of failure to face the harsh realities of economic survival, after euphoric statements about Britain's future and the promise that Utopia can be achieved painlessly, and without effort, will or sacrifice, after years of living in a fool's paradise, can the people now face the discordant music of truth?

One of the hallmarks of Margaret Thatcher's leadership is her honesty, her unswerving desire and invariable practice to tell the truth. She gives people the facts simply, without guile or equivocation. But it is one thing to tell the truth, quite another to act upon it with the inherent risk of unpopularity. And there is a gradual realisation across the whole spectrum of society that not only does Margaret Thatcher mean what she says, but she actually intends to practise what she preaches. Gone are the days of hypocrisy. To some, this is a most startling innovation in British politics.

Margaret Thatcher has never pretended that the road ahead would be easy. She didn't promise a painless path to the attainment of success. As she has said on several occasions, 'Some things will get worse before they get better, but after almost any major operation you feel worse before you convalesce. It will most certainly take time for our policies to work through but we are taking very firm action to get things right for the future.'

After just over a year of what has been frequently referred to as the 'Thatcher experiment', can we really expect a complete transformation in our fortunes – can we really expect a magic wand to wave all our troubles away? As Sir John Greenborough, who was President of the CBI until May 1980 and is now Deputy President, said, 'Margaret Thatcher has only had just over one year out of five to try and stop the economic decline which has been in the system of this country for twenty-five, maybe thirty years. I would like to feel she is going to be given every chance to see it through. I believe that after a couple of years, when the message she is preaching is driven home, when people realise there isn't a soft option, *we are going* to get

230

the response. In my view there is no alternative strategy to the one Margaret Thatcher is pursuing. If the Labour Party had been returned to power and had pursued their particular brand of policies we wouldn't be exactly bankrupt, but we would be back with our begging bowl to the IMF.

'Since the end of 1976, this country in relation to its international competitors, has become 70 per cent less effective in unit labour costs. Of that 70 per cent only 25 per cent is due to the exchange rate. We have been paying ourselves more than we earn and that is the fundamental problem in this country!

'When I first went to Europe, people were looking at our economic track record and I wasn't allowed to feel particularly proud in representing my country – I found that a source of great sadness. Now when I go to Europe the top industrialists say with great admiration, "My God, you have dedicated, driving, committed political leadership! Unless you make it with all you have going for you now, none of us are going to make it."

'I personally believe in the great future of this country. Indeed, I'm very optimistic after a bit of choppy water for the next year or two.'

Harsh decisions have already been taken, and undoubtedly harsh decisions will have to be taken in the future – it is an inevitable consequence of our national predicament. But can anyone seriously believe that any Prime Minister, any government, actually enjoys implementing unpopular measures, actually enjoys cutting public expenditure?

It takes courage to steel yourself against giant waves of unpopularity and abuse. It doesn't take courage to spend more and more public money, money we haven't earned, on highly sensitive, emotive and popular causes.

Paul Johnson, in a recent article urging the faint-hearted to stand firm against the inevitable storm clouds, commented: 'The sad truth is that Britain does not have a choice of remedies. The Government is applying the only one which is compatible with a free-enterprise economy and a parliamentary democracy ... Margaret Thatcher is

231

offering our free-enterprise system its last chance to prove it can deliver.'

On countless occasions, Margaret Thatcher has emphasised that the Trade Unions have an enormous contribution to make if only they would make it. She has persistently stressed her faith in the workers on the shop floor and in the vast majority of the British work force. In office she has shown a strikingly unshakeable belief in the British people which refuses to be daunted by demonstrations of hatred by 'Rentamob'.

Of course, all political leaders are subjected to ruthless and deeply analytical criticism, and as Margaret Thatcher said,'It's right that people should subject what you are doing to a critical faculty.' But there is a difference between criticism motivated by a genuine antipathy and difference of opinion to criticism born out of hatred and a desire to destroy. It is a sad comment on British society that too often hard work, initiative, talent and enthusiasm, together with the attendant trappings of success, are looked upon with suspicion and envy – almost hatred.

As a nation, we have become increasingly prone to pouring scorn upon the successful elements in our society. We have seemingly become too preoccupied with the reasons for failure, too little with the attainment of success.

Trade Union hostility, I suspect, is in part attributable to the fact that the Leadership has become unaccustomed to playing anything less than a major role in the formulation of Government policy. It is a source of considerable concern and surprise that the 'Iron Lady', unlike her predecessors, refuses to be influenced or intimidated by threats of strike action.

As Sir John Greenborough, whose predominant communication is with the 'Neddy Six', says, 'In Margaret Thatcher they see somebody who is utterly determined, they see somebody who is not going to be easily influenced to turn away from the path she believes to be right for the ultimate prosperity of this country. They probably see somebody who is prepared to resign before she would engage in U-turning because she is so basically dedicated.'

The Prime Minister's words at the Press Association's annual lunch echo that view: 'No great goal was ever easily achieved. But it is because we care passionately about the future of our country and its people that we are resolved to go on striving. My colleague and I will not be deflected. there can be no U-turns along *this* road – be very sure of that!'

It is perhaps the strength of her determination and the intensity of her dedication that strikes fear into the hearts of her opponents. It is my belief that Margaret Thatcher has a strong sense of destiny, perhaps reminiscent of Winston Churchill when he said 'I felt as if I were walking with destiny, and that all my past life had been but a preparation for this hour and this trial.' She is a spirited, exciting politician with an extraordinary sense of purpose who will not be deflected from her beliefs by the use of intimidatory forces.

There are those who decry Mrs Thatcher's beliefs, but not even her most vehement critics would question her sincerity and commitment. She is passionately fighting for the dignity and responsibility of the individual and the resurgence of the nation.

In my view, Margaret Thatcher is giving us our last chance for a worthwhile future, a last chance for the individual to shape his or her own life, a last chance to live by all the best values which once made this country the envy of the world, a last chance to say that 'The State is the servant and not the master of this nation'.

The last chance.

Index

Index

237

Prior, James, MP, 147, 152, 172, 182, 190–1, 222

Raphael, Adam, 126, 147
Roberts, Alfred, JP, 9–15, 18, 20, 22–4, 27–8, 29, 30, 32, 33–4, 37
Roberts, Beatrice Ethel (née Stevenson), 9–13, 20, 22–3, 28, 32
Roberts, Muriel, 10, 16, 17, 18, 22
Rowland, Peter, 53–7

Shinwell, Lord, MP, 87–90, 95
Social Democrats, 153, 155, 157, 161, 182
Somerville College, Oxford, 18, 20–1, 30–1, 36–8
Steel, David, MP, 190
Stewart, Michael, 96
Strachey, John, 99–100
Summerskill, Edith, Baroness, 96

Taylor, Edward, MP, 124–5, 135
Thatcher, Carol, 47–52, 58, 63–4, 199–200
Thatcher, Major Denis, 33, 41, 45–7, 50, 63, 188, 194, 196, 199, 211
Thatcher, Margaret Hilda (née Roberts), MA, BSc., MP, b.(1925); childhood, 9–14; education, 15–19, 25–7, 29–33; University (1943–6), 18, 20–1, 30–1, 36–8; research chemist (1947–51), 39, 41, 91; candidate (1948–51), 40–5, 91, 103; marriage (1951), 46–7; motherhood, 48–52; Lincolns Inn (1953), 48, 53–7,

103–4, 162; MP Finchley (1959), 56–7, 104; Min. P. & N.I. (1961–4), 111, 116; Shadow Min. Educ. (1969), 66; Hon. Fellow Somerville (1970); Min. Educ. (1970–74), 59, 67, 109, 134, 153, 162; MP Barnet, Finchley (1974); Leader Opposition (1975–79), 61–4, 68–75, 77, 79–80, 89, 95, 104–5, 107, 117, 120, 144–5, 175; Prime Minister (1979), 123–233 quoted, 178–80, 184–5, 195–216
Thatcher, Mark, 48–52, 58–64, 194, 197, 199, 200
Thorneycroft, Lord, 121–32, 136, 149, 150, 229
Trotskyites, 101–2

Villiers, Sir Charles, 222

Walden, Brian, ITV, 75–87, 131, 154, 170, 173, 181–2
Walpole, Sir Robert, 128
Warrender, Victor, MP, 19
Whitelaw, William, MP, 112, 116–21, 172, 188
Wickstead, Margaret (née Goodrich), 29–33, 38
Williams, Shirley, 96, 130
Wilson, Sir Harold, MP, 65, 68, 74, 77, 94–102, 151, 156, 192
women, MP's, 68–9, 89, 95–6, 102, 104, 106–8, 116, 139
Woodhouse, Monty, MP, 111
Woollcott, Mr & Mrs, 41–2
Woolton, Lord, 122